The Joy of Truffles

evergreen

EVERGREEN is an imprint of Benedikt Taschen Verlag GmbH

© 1998 Benedikt Taschen Verlag GmbH
Hohenzollernring 53, D–50672 Köln
Conception: Patrik Jaros, Raffaella und Raoul Manuel Schnell
Photography: Raffaella and Raoul Manuel Schnell
Texts: Otward Buchner
Recipes and foodstyling: Patrik Jaros
Design: Susanne Schaal
Translation: Christian Goodden, Bungay
Edited by Yvonne Havertz, Cologne

Printed in Italy
ISBN 3-8228-7632-1

Tout est mystère, magie,
sortilège, tout ce qui
s'accomplit entre le
moment de poser
sur le feu la cocotte,
le coquemar, la
marmite et leur
contenu, et le moment
plein de douce
anxiété, de voluptueux
espoir, où vous décoiffez
sur la table le
plat fumant .....

Prologue with truffle, man and poor pig

A pig strikes lucky. It finds a truffle. End of its good fortune – enter man. He snatches away the tantalizing tuber from under the very snout of the desperately rooting pig and gets a lot of money for it (truffles: £1 000 a kilo).

The pig gets a banal turnip (turnips: £0.60 a kilo) and can perhaps count itself lucky that it will live to see another year. I ask you: is that fair? It is. Maybe not from the porker's point of view, but certainly from the perspective of the gourmet. Anyone who has fallen under the spell of the truffle will not – with the best will in the world – see why a pig of all animals should have the pleasure of eating this hideous, knobbly, pitted, but divine-tasting fungal fruit. Yes, that's the way gourmets are. Prepared even to buy this book, to read it and to cook from it. But it is not meant to be to your disadvantage, quite the reverse.

The truffle –
a mystery?

The truffle has had a chequered history stretching back to antiquity. It has been a mineral, a plant created by thunder and lightning, and – as ascetic clerics put it about in the Middle Ages – a monstrous creation of the devil. In the meantime we have grown a bit wiser. The truffle belongs to the species of ascomycetous fungi. Actually, what has us rolling our eyes and searching for words (more later) is not the fungus, but its fruiting body or the result of subterranean sexuality. The actual fungus is a ramifying network of hyphae threads that extend many metres in the ground – the fungus's mycelium. When the hyphae of different fungal branches meet, the result is the tuber in question. In our case a truffle – assuming the weather has been clement and the soil contains humus and chalk. What makes the matter even more complicated and makes cultivation correspondingly ticklish is the phenomenon of mycorrhiza. This is the close symbiotic relationship that the filament networks of fungi and tree roots enter into.

A regular two-way trade goes on between them. The truffle supplies nitrogen, phosphorus, potassium and similar goodies, while the tree reciprocates with carbohydrates. But the truffle does not enter into this arrangement with just any old tree. No, it must be a maple, a birch, a lime or an elm. Most of all it likes to cohabit with the oak, a liaison which we can thank for the aromatic truffle.

Incidentally, the truffle's name stems from the fact that it sets up home – inconsiderately – some 5 to 30 cms deep in the ground. This can cause the surface above it to rise slightly, a lifting that mediaeval people came to describe with the late Latin term 'terrae tuffolae'. Later this became progressively contracted and transformed into 'tartuffole', 'tartufo' (Italian), 'truffe' (French) and 'truffle' (English).

The truffle – a delicate diva

Truffles are very sensitive to the weather. Hard winter frosts and dry summers are the ruination of a truffle. In particular August must be wet, warm and full of thunderstorms. August is the making of a truffle. And also, unfortunately, of wine. Which leads to a surprising observation. A very good year for truffles is tantamount to a bad vintage. For wine likes moderately humid-to-dry conditions in the period August-October.

Thus in 1986, an excellent year for wine in France, Gallic truffle production slumped from about 100 tons to 20. The year 1987, by contrast, saw a disastrous vintage but the truffle crop of the century. Poetic justice!

Tuber melanosporum vittadini

Tuber magnatum pico

The truffle – an aroma that gets under your skin

There's no getting round it. In the next few lines we are going to have to call a spade a spade. In some quarters, that would lead to people screwing up their noses, and in others to some polite rephrasing, which would be right and decorous, but which in the end would be wide of the mark. We are talking here of the truffle's smell, its aroma. Besides many other nuances of smell, such as garlic, the truffle has, so it is said, animal hints – something musky, sensual, even erotic.

And all are directed to the same end: to beguile us, the truffle pig, the truffle dog and the truffle goat. The substance responsible for this, which accounts for much of the truffle's mystery, is testosterase, a substance almost identical with the sexual hormone testosterone, which is also present in male sperm and helps give it its characteristic smell. This explains too the enthusiastic rooting of the truffle-hunting sow. She divines powerfully and instinctively the scent of a boar. The truffle does not have the same aphrodisiac effect on us humans, as is commonly supposed. Nevertheless, it touches a subliminal autonomic area in us. Eating truffles can be an exciting experience ...

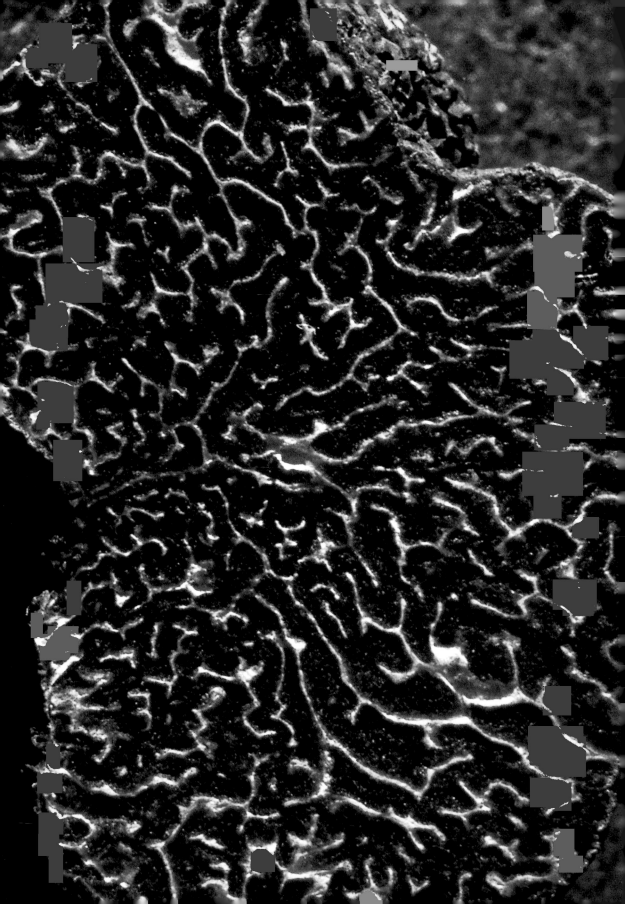

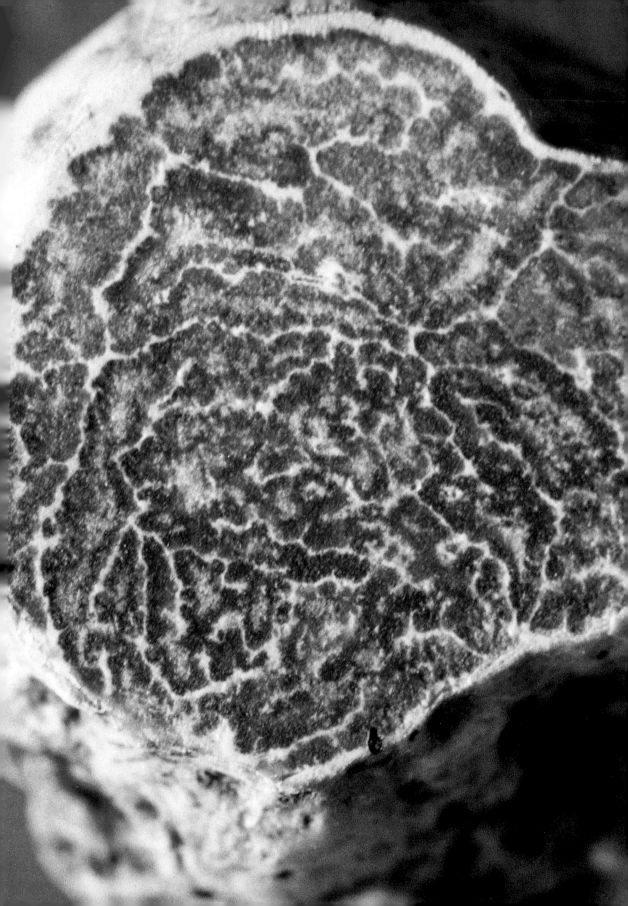

A brief history
of the truffle

Love of the truffle extends back into the mists of time. We know for sure that a certain Mr Cheops, the incumbent pharaoh 4 600 years ago, prized it. And 2 000 years later a Mr Licinius, the Roman governor of Carthage, apparently lost two teeth when biting into one – at least that is what Pliny narrates. The ancient Greeks and Romans were considered particular aficionados of the truffle. After the collapse of the Roman empire, a black hole opens up in truffle history. The truffle, with its aphrodisiac smell, was anathema to the ascetic churchmen of mediaeval times. Only when man was "resurrected", when the Renaissance came along, did the truffle come back into fashion. And then with a vengeance. All the European royal houses were enamoured of it, and Maria Theresa was downright smitten by the tuber, which she liked incorporated into an omelette.

"Homo tuberensis" – the truffle hunter

How can you spot a truffle hunter? Well, at first you can't. His – and except in France it is a man's job – is a clandestine occupation that shuns the limelight and other people. Unless the truffle hunter is among his own kind. Then he has plenty to say, although much of it is designed to put his fellow seekers and rivals on the wrong track. After all, a truffle grove is a pot of gold. Perhaps you can recognize the truffle hunter by his hands, which have shifted many a barrowload of earth, or perhaps by his dog, which he values inordinately.

One thing you can't immediately recognize is his intuition, his knowledge of complex arcane inter-relations between the soil, the air and the weather. This enables him to stop and delve where the likes of us would dumbly pass by.

Perhaps you can recognize him by his cunning, his shiftiness.

After all, he has to fool his rivals, the taxman and from time to time a customer. No, it is not easy to unmask a "Homo tuberensis". But once you have got to know one, you can't imagine him as anything else – other than as a truffle hunter.

Starters (Hors d'œuvres)

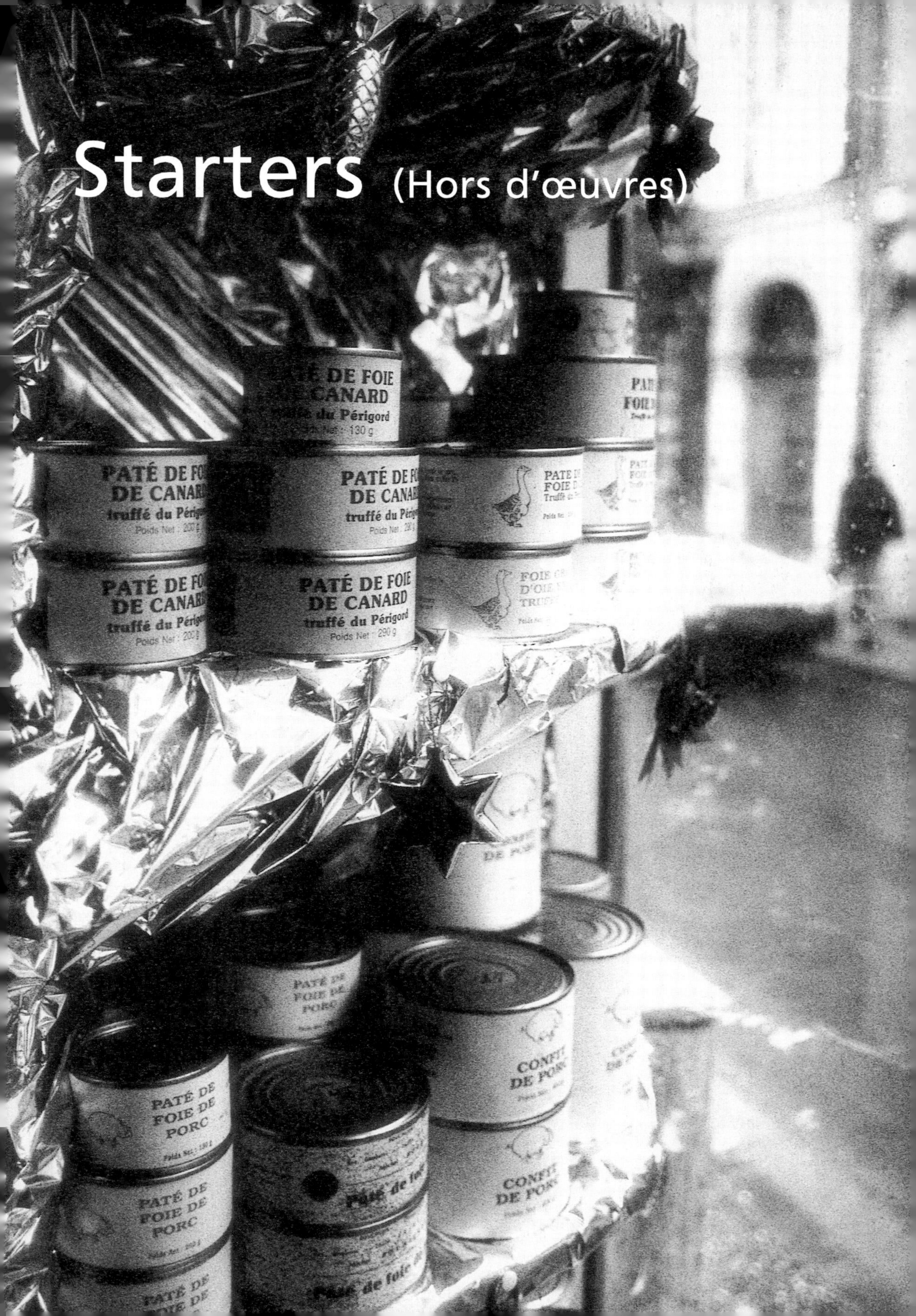

Endive with raw artichokes and poulard liver

Trim off top two thirds of the artichokes. Cut back stalk to 2 cm (1"). Remove the outer green leaves, and scrape out the choke with a small spoon and discard. Reserve artichokes in lemon water for further preparation.

Pluck endive into bite-sized pieces and wash. Likewise pluck parsley leaves from their stalks. Prepare vinaigrette of olive oil, lemon juice, salt, icing sugar and white pepper.

Remove any membranes from chicken liver, and fry liver in butter in a small pan. Season with salt and white pepper. Cut artichokes into wafer-thin slices and toss in vinaigrette along with endive and parsley leaves. Arrange on plates, placing pieces of fried chicken liver on salad. Sprinkle with sliced white truffle and grated Parmesan. Ill. pp. 26–27.

Serves 4

Ingredients
1 endive
6 globe artichokes
1 bunch flat-leaf parsley
40 g grated Parmesan cheese
200 g poulard (fattened chicken) liver – this is much paler and finer than normal chicken liver
20 g butter
40 g white truffle

Vinaigrette
8 tbsp extra virgin olive oil
juice of one lemon
salt
pinch of icing sugar
white pepper

Lukewarm marinated leeks in truffle vinaigrette

Trim off dark green part of leeks and discard. Halve leeks and wash thoroughly. Boil for about 10 minutes in plenty of salted water. Leeks should not be too crunchy or they will be too peppery. Briefly refresh in ice-cold salted water, removing immediately. Marinate with the truffle vinaigrette while still lukewarm.

A very simple but fantastic dish. In France it is served not only as a starter, but also for supper, accompanied by some sour cream and thick hunks of bread. Ill. p. 31.

Serves 4

Ingredients
8 young leeks
150 ml truffle vinaigrette
(see "Stocks and Sauces")

Ingredients

1 firm medium-sized lettuce
1 romanesco
2 hard-boiled eggs
1 bunch dill
80 g black summer truffle

Dressing

3 tbsp crème fraîche
3 tbsp cream
2 tbsp white wine vinegar
2 tbsp lemon juice
salt
cayenne pepper
4 tbsp extra virgin olive oil

Lettuce with romanesco and black summer truffle

Divide up the romanesco into florets and boil in salted water until crisp-tender. Refresh in ice-cold water and drain. Wash lettuce, divide into bite-sized pieces and shake or spin dry. Shell and finely chop hard-boiled eggs.

Prepare a creamy dressing with crème fraîche, cream, white wine vinegar, salt, cayenne pepper and olive oil, and marinate the romanesco florets in it. Place lettuce leaves on plate. Arrange romanesco florets among them. Garnish with chopped egg, dill tips and sliced summer truffle. Dribble remaining dressing over lettuce. A wonderfully fresh summer salad that can also be served as an evening meal. Ill. p. 35.

Serves 4

Beetroot salad with black truffle and sour cream

Remove leaves from beetroot. Boil in water seasoned with sugar, salt, caraway and cider vinegar until soft. Allow to cool and rub off skins under running water with your fingers. Cut beetroot carpaccio-wise into very thin slices. Marinate in a vinaigrette made of cider vinegar, salt, sugar, black pepper and sunflower oil.

Clean and wash oak-leaf lettuce, and pluck into small pieces. Also marinate in vinaigrette, and then assemble a small bouquet in centre of plate. Arrange a garland of beetroot slices around oak-leaf lettuce leaves. Scatter truffle strips over salad, drizzle with remaining vinaigrette, and garnish with sour cream. Ill. pp. 36–37.

Serves 4

Ingredients
300 g fresh beetroot
1 tsp caraway
salt
sugar
a good splash of cider vinegar
1 small oak-leaf lettuce

Salad
60 g fine strips of black truffle
8 tbsp cold-pressed sunflower oil
5 tbsp cider vinegar
salt
pinch of icing sugar
freshly ground black pepper
100 g sour cream

Pan-fried breast of guinea fowl with stuffed artichoke hearts and white truffle

Ingredients
2 small guinea fowl weighing
approx. 600 g each
salt
30 g butter
2 tbsp brown chicken sauce
(see "Stocks and Sauces")

Artichoke hearts
8 small globe artichokes
2 tbsp olive oil for frying
1 clove of garlic, unpeeled
1 sprig of thyme
2 sticks of white celery
2 tbsp mayonnaise
juice of half a lemon
cayenne pepper
a few dashes of Worcestershire
sauce
white celery leaves
40 g white truffle

Remove breasts and legs from guinea fowl. Season legs and roast in oven for about 25 minutes skin side down. Separate meat from bones, allow to cool and dice small.

Chop celery raw into small cubes. Mix with meat from legs, dress with mayonnaise, and season with lemon juice, cayenne pepper and Worcestershire sauce.

Trim off top two thirds of artichokes and all the stalks. Remove tough outer green leaves, scrape out choke with a small spoon and discard. Lightly fry leaves in olive oil with garlic clove and sprig of thyme, not allowing them to take on too much colour. Sprinkle with lemon juice and allow to cool. Stuff with celery and guinea-fowl salad, and arrange on a plate.

Meanwhile pan-fry guinea fowl breasts (skinless) in butter. Add some chicken sauce to the pan and baste. Arrange guinea fowl breasts and stuffed artichokes on a plate. Garnish with celery leaves and slice truffle on top to taste. Ill. p. 43.

Serves 4

"Mousse à la Fage"
Coarse venison mousse with pâté de foie gras and port aspic

Heat half the butter until frothy. Add the apple and lightly glaze with sugar. Add venison and brown slightly. Add orange zest, juniper berries, bay leaves and thyme. Mix in Madeira and cognac, and reduce. Pour in veal sauce, and cook the venison for about 30 minutes, covered. Remove meat, strain sauce through a fine sieve, and add chopped truffles to the sauce. Rapidly sauté chicken liver in remaining butter and add Grand Marnier. Mince venison, cooked pork belly, foie gras and chicken liver in a meat mincer (fine setting) and pass through a fine sieve. In a bowl, stir in the sauce while still warm, season generously, and carefully fold in whipped cream. Transfer to a terrine and allow to cool for two hours. Decorate with slices of truffle and pour port aspic on top. Mousse tastes best after resting for two days. Serve with brioches. Ill. pp. 46–47.

Serves 10

Ingredients
350 g lean haunch of venison, trimmed
220 g smoked belly of pork, cooked
180 g chicken liver
120 g raw pâté de foie gras
40 g butter
120 g apple segments
30 g sugar
1 strip of orange zest
1/2 tsp crushed juniper berries
1 sprig of thyme
2 bay leaves
1/4 l brown veal (or venison) sauce (see "Stocks and Sauces")
6 cl Madeira
4 cl cognac
2 cl Grand Marnier
salt
white pepper
350 ml whipped cream
60 g black truffle, chopped small
80 g black truffle, sliced
1/4 l basic aspic jelly (see "Stocks and Sauces"), seasoned with red port

Which way to the truffle, please?

The demanding cocktail of climate, soil and flora that pleases His Excellency the truffle severely curtails the area of its distribution. Broadly speaking, this lies between the 40th and 47th parallels, and cuts a swathe from Touraine, via Libourne and Périgord, past the Mediterranean, to the Italian border, with a bulge into the Rhône valley. In Italy the swathe continues from Alba and follows the Apennines down to the latitude of Rome. On the Iberian peninsula truffles can be found* south of the Pyrenees as far as Guadalajara.

*Remarkably, truffle hunting and cultivation are a man's occupation.

...tornavano insanguati,
morti, ma carichi;
di pernici, di lepri,
di selvaggina...

Ingredients for about 30 small
fritters

Soufflé fritters
125 ml milk
125 ml water
100 g butter
1/4 tsp salt
**170 g sifted plain flour – 405
high-gluten type**
5 eggs

Truffle mousse
**500 g best back ham, trimmed
of rind and fat**
200 ml crème fraîche
**150 ml dissolved basic aspic jelly
(see "Stocks and Sauces")**
10 g butter
150 g finely chopped black truffle
6 cl old Madeira
250 ml whipped cream
salt
freshly ground white pepper

Soufflé fritters filled
with black truffle mousse

Dice ham and purée in a blender. Slowly pour in dissolved aspic jelly, and fold in crème fraîche. Sweat the chopped truffle in butter, pour in Madeira and add to ham mixture. Season and carefully fold in whipped cream. Allow to cool for at least 2 hours.

Bring milk, water, butter and salt to the boil, then remove from stove. Stir in sifted flour with a whisk. Continue to stir paste with a wooden spoon until it lifts from bottom of pan, leaving a white film there. Transfer paste to a bowl and gradually work in eggs, taking care that dough does not go lumpy, which can happen if too much egg is added at once.

Line a baking tray with grease-proof paper and preheat oven to 220 °C. Using a piping bag, squeeze out dollops 2 cm wide and put in oven. Pour out half a coffee cup of water in oven – the steam from this makes the soufflé fritters rise properly. After 10 minutes, open oven door slightly so that the steam can escape and the fritters become nice and crisp. Leave fritters to cool. Then, using a piping bag, inject them with truffle mousse. Makes a perfect accompaniment to a glass of champagne served to guests as an aperitif.

Raw veal olives stuffed with curd cheese and white truffle

Ingredients
200 g curd cheese
50 g sour cream
salt
white pepper
a few drops of white truffle oil
16 very thin slices of fresh veal fillet
16 raw spinach leaves, evenly sized
4 tbsp extra virgin olive oil
coarse salt
40 g white truffle

Mix curd cheese with sour cream and season with salt, white pepper and truffle oil. Place raw spinach leaves on slices of veal fillet, and stuff with the curd cheese mixture. Roll into small olives and place four side by side on each plate. Season with coarse salt and drizzle with olive oil. Finally, garnish with slices of white truffle and serve with lightly toasted white bread.

Serves 4

Mousse d'

la Fage

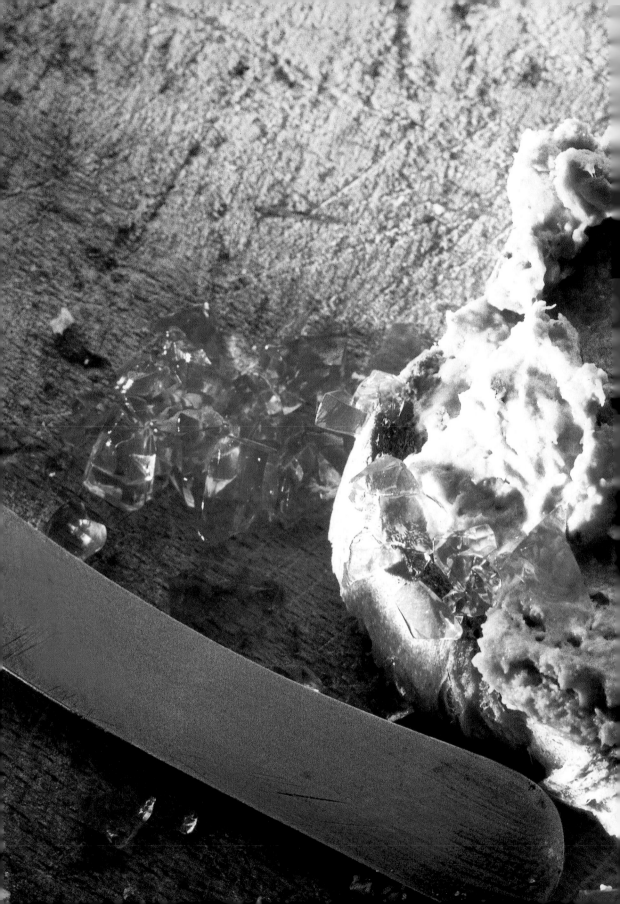

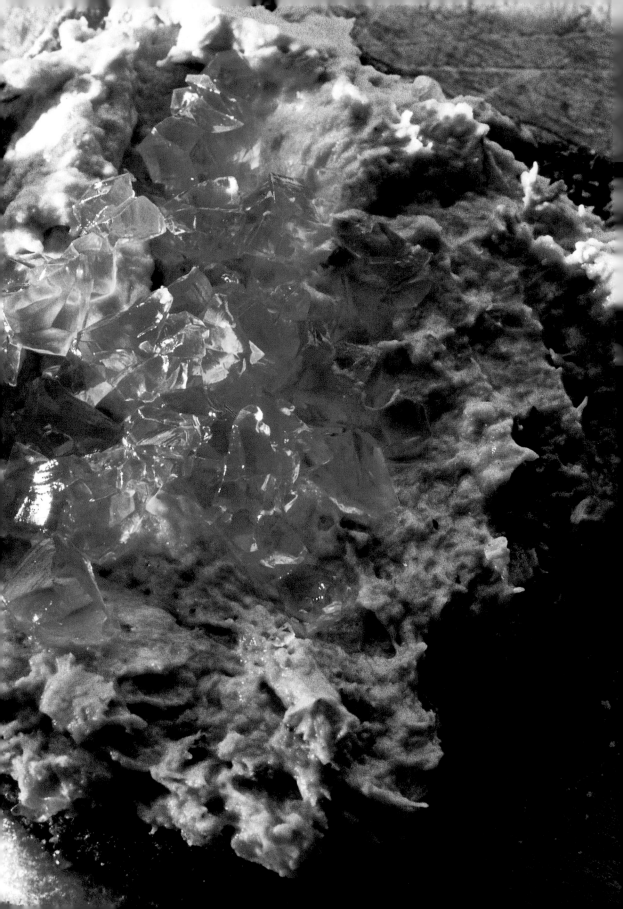

Carpaccio of beef
with summer truffles

Ingredients
**1 beef fillet weighing about
1.2 kg, trimmed and shaped
60 g black summer truffle
30 g freshly grated young
Parmesan
80 ml extra virgin olive oil
four drops white truffle oil
juice of one lemon
cracked black pepper
coarse salt**

For this recipe, use not well-hung but absolutely fresh beef fillet. Thoroughly wrap meat in cling film without dicing it, and freeze.

Mix together olive oil, truffle oil and lemon juice, and spread one tablespoonful on a flat plate. Slice beef wafer-thin in a slicing machine and arrange on plate. Spread another tablespoonful of the oil mixture over the slices.

Slice the black summer truffle over the carpaccio. Season with coarse salt and freshly cracked black pepper. Finally sprinkle some finely grated young Parmesan over the carpaccio and drizzle with more oil. Serve with fresh white bread.

If you do not have a slicing machine at home, you can resort to a simple trick. With a sharp knife, cut the beef fillet (unfrozen) into slices 2mm thick, place them between two frozen coolbags, and beat very thin with a steak hammer. Then prepare as described above.

Serves 4

Truffled parfait
of chicken liver

Line terrine first with cling film and then with thin slices of green speck bacon so that the speck overlaps the edges by about 5 cm. Set terrine aside and chill. Heat butter until whey is golden and butter has a nutty taste – noisette butter.

Steep chicken liver in milk for four hours to draw out most of its bitter substances. Remove and trim off any veins or membranes.

Sweat chopped truffle in a little butter, add Madeira and port, and together with herbs and spices reduce to $1/3$ of its original volume. Remove herbs and spices.

Using a hand blender, purée liver with eggs (yokes and whites). Mix in the still warm noisette butter. Season and – now using only an egg whisk – stir in the reduced truffle mixture. Transfer to prepared terrine and seal in with bacon ends. Cover with a lid, place in a double-saucepan, and cook for about 35 minutes in an oven at 120 °C. Take out and chill in refrigerator overnight.

Ingredients for a terrine
holding approx. 1 kg
450 g fresh chicken liver
2 eggs
400 g butter
100 g black truffle, chopped
150 ml Madeira
200 ml port (red)
1 sprig of thyme
1 bay leaf
5 juniper berries
a pinch of pickling salt –
ask your butcher
salt
freshly milled white pepper
100 g green (speck) bacon,
thinly sliced

Soups and stews

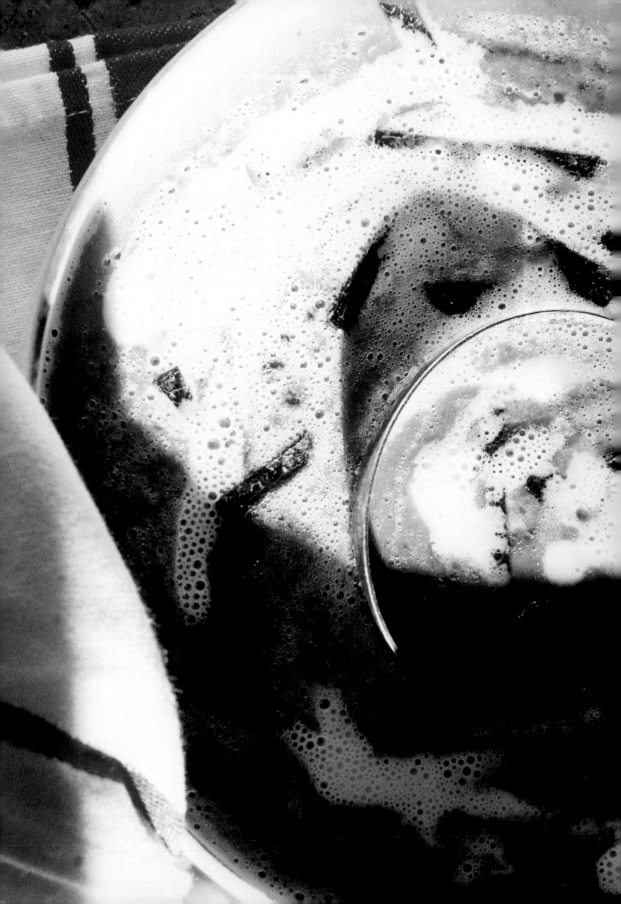

Ingredients

**150 g sweet chestnuts,
cooked and peeled**
40 g celery
40 g celeriac
20 g speck bacon strips
20 g butter
2 cl Madeira
3 juniper berries
1 bay leaf
**3/4 l chicken stock
(see "Stocks and Sauces")**
200 ml cream
1 tbsp whipped cream

Garnish

60 g broad strips of black truffle
10 g butter
**2 tbsp brown veal sauce
(see "Stocks and Sauces")**

Cream of chestnut soup
with black truffle strips

Slowly render down the speck in butter. Dice celery and celeriac, and put in peeled chestnuts. Add herbs and spices, and pour in chicken stock. Allow soup to simmer for 15 minutes. Improve with cream, liquidize and pass through a fine conical strainer. Reheat, and stir in the whipped cream. Soften truffle strips in butter, add brown veal sauce, and garnish soup stripwise with truffle and sauce. Ill. pp. 54–55.

Serves 4

Essence of calf's tail with truffled semolina dumplings

Prepare essence as described and reserve. Beat soft butter with salt, white pepper and nutmeg until fluffy. Add chopped truffle to butter. Gradually stir in eggs, not allowing mixture to go lumpy. Briskly mix in semolina with a wooden spoon, and cut out small dumplings with two teaspoons. Place in boiling water, cover, and simmer gently for 12 to 15 minutes. Remove and add to hot essence. Garnish with flat-leaf parsley if desired, and serve piping hot. Ill. p. 59.

Serves 8

Ingredients
To make the essence, use the same recipe as for basic aspic jelly (see "Stocks and Sauces") except that, instead of calves' hoofs, you use pieces of already seared calf's tail.

Dumplings
100 g soft butter
2 small eggs
200 g durum wheat semolina
60 g black truffle, finely chopped
salt
white pepper
freshly grated nutmeg

Ingredients
200 g white haricot beans, softened
120 g white onion, sliced
40 g butter
1 bay leaf
1 l chicken stock
(see "Stocks and Sauces")
250 g crème fraîche
freshly ground black pepper

Garnish
2 hard-boiled eggs
40 g black truffle, sliced
10 g butter
2 cl Madeira

Strained white bean soup with chopped egg

Sweat onion in butter until translucent. Add soaked beans, bay leaf and chicken stock, and simmer gently for 35 minutes. Remove bay leaf, add crème fraîche, season with black pepper, and liquidize.

Strain through a fine sieve and serve in soup bowls. Garnish soup with chopped egg and truffle slices pre-softened in butter and Madeira. Finally, fold another spoonful of crème fraîche into the hot soup. Ill. p. 63.

Serves 4

"Ceci alla Piemontese"
Cabbage stew with chick peas and white truffle

Sweat sliced onion and shredded cabbage in olive oil, add chick peas and bacon, and pour in beef or chicken stock. Add bay leaf and simmer gently for 30 minutes. The stew is ready when the chick peas begin to disintegrate. Finally, add the parsley and white pepper, and, if necessary, adjust seasoning by adding more salt.

Sprinkle slices of bread with cheese and lightly brown in a hot oven. Put gratinéd slices in soup bowls and pour hot soup over them. Slice the white truffle on top and serve. Ill. pp. 68–69.

Serves 4–6

Ingredients
600 g savoy cabbage, coarsely cut
140 g chick peas, soaked
50 g onion, sliced
80 g speck bacon
60 ml olive oil
10 small slices country-style rye bread
180 g grated fontina (cheese from the Aosta valley)
1 1/2 l beef or chicken stock (see "Stocks and Sauces")
1 bay leaf
salt
white pepper
1/2 bunch of parsley
40–60 g white truffle

Bean ragout
with cotechino sausages

Ingredients
280 g mixed red beans – soaked
for 2 hours in cold water
150 g brunoise of carrot, celery
and shallot (diced small)
1/2 clove of garlic, crushed
30 g olive oil
20 g butter
1 sprig of rosemary
30 g tomato purée
1 bay leaf
2 large sage leaves for flavouring
1 l chicken stock
(see "Stocks and Sauces")
salt
freshly milled black pepper

Garnish
8 red cotechini (coarse, highly-
spiced Italian sausages)
20 ml olive oil
40 g white truffle

Sweat vegetable brunoise and garlic in a mixture of olive oil and butter. Add bay leaf, sage leaves, rosemary and red beans. Add tomato purée, pour in chicken stock and gently simmer, not letting the beans disintegrate. Remove rosemary, sage and bay leaf, and check seasoning.

Slowly fry cotechini in olive oil and allow to infuse in finished bean ragout. Season with freshly ground black pepper. Serve bean stew with two cotechini per person, and sprinkle with sliced white truffle. Round off completed dish with a few drops of best olive oil. Ill. pp. 66–67.

Serves 4

Cream of semolina soup with white truffle

Lightly fry soft wheat semolina in 75 g of melted butter until semolina takes on a pale yellow colour. Add shallot and immediately pour in chicken stock. This soup must be constantly stirred so that it does not catch on the pan. Simmer slowly for about 10 minutes, checking seasoning. Heat remaining butter until whey becomes golden (noisette butter). Serve soup, sprinkle with freshly grated Parmesan and sliced white truffle, and finally dribble noisette butter over the finished soup. This is an unjustly neglected dish, as the thick consistency of the soup goes splendidly with white truffle.

Serves 4

Ingredients
120 g soft wheat semolina
75 g butter
30 g shallot, diced small
1 l chicken stock
(see "Stocks and Sauces")
freshly ground black pepper
salt
40 g freshly grated Parmesan
30 g butter
50 g white truffle

Risotto Piemontese

Ingredients
350 g pumpkin, coarsely diced
60 g leek
80 g celeriac
1/2 red pepper
1/2 clove of garlic
30 g butter
20 g tomato purée
1 small sprig of thyme
1/2 bay leaf
1 tsp sweet paprika powder
1/2 tsp curry powder
a few dashes of cider vinegar
3/4 l chicken stock
(see "Stocks and Sauces")
150 ml cream
a pinch of cayenne pepper
salt
freshly grated nutmeg
40 g white truffle

Cream of pumpkin and paprika soup

Chop up leek, celeriac, garlic and red pepper, and sweat in butter. Add pumpkin chunks and cook until liquid has almost boiled away. Add tomato purée and dust with paprika powder. Immediately add a few dashes of cider vinegar to stop paprika becoming bitter. Add thyme and bay leaf, and pour in chicken stock. Simmer gently for 15 minutes, liquidize and strain through a fine sieve. Season with cayenne pepper and nutmeg, fold in cream, and do not allow to cook any more. Serve soup in deep bowls and slice truffles to taste over the soup.

Serves 4

Cream of celery soup
with black Périgord truffle

Peel and coarsely dice celeriac and boil for a few minutes in salted water. Drain and refresh in cold water.

Fry diced shallot in foaming butter until translucent, add drained celeriac cubes and splash in a few dashes of cider vinegar. Pour in chicken stock, season and gently simmer for about 15 minutes. Add cream and bring back to boil. Liquidize in a blender and strain through a fine sieve. Season with freshly grated nutmeg to taste and serve.

Carefully peel truffle and cut up into thin slices. Briefly heat in foaming butter and add Madeira. Serve soup in bowls, float sweated truffle slices on top of soup, and dribble in truffle juices.

Serves 4

Ingredients
400 g celeriac
2 shallots, finely chopped
40 g butter
a few dashes of cider vinegar
salt
freshly grated nutmeg
600 ml chicken stock
(see "Stocks and Sauces")
200 ml single cream

Garnish
1 black Périgord truffle weighing
approx. 50 g
20 g butter
40 cl old Madeira

The truffle markets – turning tubers into dough

If you've never been taken for a ride, here in the truffle markets you can make up for lost time. Dealers can smell a layman like the pig smells a truffle. The finest tubers you won't see anyway. They are snapped up by the middlemen working for the large delicatessens and restaurants. Cut.

A car park. Chill morning mist swirls over the broken asphalt. Two cars emerge out of the gloom, crunch over the gravel, and draw up. Three men get out. Numbers, prices are muttered. French? Italian? It doesn't matter. Repeatedly the men look round them, probing the mist with their eyes.
One of them silently opens the boot of his vehicle. Briefly his upper body disappears into its cavernous

mouth. He fishes out a number of plastic bags, out of which the other two extract dark fist-sized nuggets. They inspect them, smell them, turn them over in their fingers and, satisfied, pat the supplier on the shoulder. Wordlessly he counts their wad of banknotes and hands over the plastic bags to them. A quick handshake, they merge back into their cars and disappear again into the mist and gloom. Cut.

This metamorphosis of fungus into money is, of course, a thorn in the flesh of the taxman. But what can he do? People close ranks and only openly trade lower-grade produce, not just for show, but to pretend poverty to the taxman. What Lalbenque is to the French, Alba is to the Italians. Two outstanding truffle markets, where the atmosphere is a bit like in a narcotics market. The better specimens lie deep in the pockets of the truffle hunters and change hands almost surreptitiously. The rest are displayed in baskets or on white linen for the ordinary citizen to ponder, who wonders where the restaurants get their "big lumps" from.

The other important markets in France are: Bergerac, Perigeux, Saint Alvère in Perigot, Richerenches, Carpentras, Valréas and Aups. In Italy the biggest are, besides Alba and Asti: Norci in Umbria and Aqualagna. The latter, incidentally, is the only place where both black and white truffles are sold.

The truffle –
a question
of price

Now, we don't want to spoil your appetite, but truffles are expensive. They cannot, strictly speaking, be cultivated – the best one can do is provide them with an ideal environment – and so they are and remain rare little creatures. A kilo of "Melanosporum" will set you back £500 and a kilo of "Magnatum" a cool £1000–2650, depending on the weather and demand. However, for a dish with white truffles all you need is about 5 g and for a dish with black truffles 20 g, which makes the price look more reasonable... Bon appétit!

Potato and egg dishes

Ingredients

300 g leaf spinach
20 g butter
1/2 tsp garlic, finely chopped
salt
white pepper
freshly grated nutmeg
100 ml double cream
4 small fresh eggs
20 g butter
cracked black pepper
80 g white truffle
2 tbsp brown veal sauce
(see "Stocks and Sauces")

Fried egg on leaf spinach with white truffle

Wash leaf spinach, briefly blanch, refresh and drain thoroughly. Sweat finely chopped garlic in butter and add spinach leaves. Season and pour in double cream. Allow to reduce somewhat.

Fry eggs in remaining butter and sprinkle with freshly cracked black pepper. Arrange spinach on plates and place fried eggs on top. Dribble on a few drops of veal sauce, and serve with plenty of sliced truffle. This dish can also be served with crisp-fried potatoes, making a marvellous complete meal. Ill. p. 82.

Serves 4

Scrambled egg
with black truffle

Ingredients
3 fresh large eggs
2 tbsp crème fraîche
20 g farm butter
50 g black truffle, sliced
salt and black pepper for seasoning at table

Briefly mix together eggs, crème fraîche and sliced black truffle, and cover well with cling film. This can be done the night before – overnight, the eggs take on a very intense truffle aroma. Heat butter until it begins to foam and add egg-truffle mixture. Stirring carefully with a wooden spatula, cook scrambled egg slowly. Scrambled egg should be neither too runny nor too solid. However, this is a matter of taste, so develop your own preferred consistency. Serve at once and season at table with salt and freshly ground black pepper. Ill. p. 83.

Serves 2

Dordogne

Oeufs speck skin

Ingredients

3/4 kg ripe pumpkin
500 g floury potatoes,
boiled in their jackets
2 fresh eggs
80 g cornflour
100 g durum wheat semolina
salt
white pepper
a pinch of sugar
freshly grated nutmeg
60 g butter
40 g white truffle

Pumpkin gnocchi
with white truffle

Cut pumpkin into slices approx. 4 cm thick. Season with salt, pepper and sugar, and wrap well in aluminium foil. Cook in a slow oven for about one hour at 190 °C. Unwrap and transfer cooked pumpkin flesh to a pan. Over a low flame, slowly boil off juices and allow to cool.

Mash potatoes in a press and mix with eggs, semolina, cornflour and pumpkin flesh to form a dough. On a floured worktop, shape dough into a roll about 2 cm in diameter and cut into 2 to 3-cm lengths, forming the gnocchi with the back of a fork. Simmer in plenty of boiling salted water, allow to stand, and refresh in cold water. Heat 40 g of butter in a pan and fry gnocchi until golden. Season with salt, pepper and nutmeg, and slice white truffle on top. Ill. pp. 88–89.

Serves 4

Gnocchi with chestnut and salsiccia sauce

Fry shallot and garlic in olive oil until translucent. Add salsiccia and mix together thoroughly with a kitchen spoon. Season with salt and pepper, and add tomato purée. Continue to fry gently, so that the sauce later takes on a nice colour. Now add small chestnuts and pour in chicken stock. Cover and cook for a further 20 minutes in the oven at 180 °C.

Mash potatoes through a press while still warm and combine with egg yoke, flour, semolina and salt to make a homogeneous dough. Roll out to about finger thickness and cut into 2-cm lengths. Form into gnocchi with the back of a fork and put into plenty of salted water. Bring to the boil, remove and allow to stand briefly. Mix straight from the water into the sauce. Serve with sage leaves tossed in hot butter. And don't forget the finely sliced white truffle! Ill. pp. 100–101.

Serves 4

Ingredients
900 g floury potatoes, boiled
150 g plain flour – 405 type
100 g semolina
2 egg yokes
salt

Sauce
250 g small chestnuts, roasted
400 g truffled salsiccia
(Italian grilled sausage)
30 g shallot, finely chopped
1/2 tsp garlic, finely chopped
1/2 tsp tomato purée
300 ml chicken stock
(see "Stocks and Sauces")
freshly ground black pepper
salt
50 ml olive oil
20 g butter
10 fresh sage leaves
60 g white truffle

"Oeufs pochés Dordogne" Poached eggs in chive vinaigrette with black truffle

Ingredients
4 fresh, very cold eggs
2 l water
50 ml white wine vinegar

Vinaigrette
2 bunches of chives
4 tbsp chicken stock
(see "Stocks and Sauces")
6 tbsp white wine vinegar
10 tbsp cold-pressed sunflower oil
white pepper
pinch sugar
30 g black truffle, sliced
10 g butter
salt

Scissor chives, combine with chicken stock, white wine vinegar, salt, white pepper and a little sugar, and liquidize with a hand-held blender. Gradually trickle in sunflower oil, season and set aside. Heat water in a saucepan until bubbles form on sides, and add vinegar. Beat egg in a ladle and slowly slide into water. With a spoon, move egg to and fro to give it a nice shape. Remove and briefly refresh in iced water. On the inside, poached eggs should be as soft as butter.

Spread vinaigrette over plate, halve poached egg, and lay on top. Heat truffle slices in melted butter and lightly season with salt. Spoon over halved eggs and, if desired, serve with a little coarse salt. Ill. pp. 86–87.

Serves 4

Souffléd eggs
with black truffle

With a serrated knife, cut off top quarter of brown eggs, collecting egg white and yokes in a bowl. Set aside for later use. Clean brown eggshells and place side by side in a bed of salt.

Sweat truffle in butter, add Madeira, and pour in brown veal sauce. Allow to reduce somewhat and share out into the eight egg shells. Separate the four white eggs, and beat the egg-white semi-stiff with a little salt and pepper. Fold in yokes and whipped cream, and likewise spoon into egg shells, taking care to leave a 1-cm-high rim at the top so the egg mixture does not spill out when it soufflés.

Place in oven preheated to 220 °C (no fan, heat only from above and below), and cook for about 3–5 minutes. Fill four small bowls with coarse salt, place two egg soufflé shells in each, and serve with small spoons. Do not use silver – it will tarnish.

Serves 4

Ingredients
8 fresh brown eggs
4 large fresh eggs
100 g black truffle,
coarsely chopped
10 g butter
2 cl Madeira
50 ml brown veal sauce
(see "Stocks and Sauces")
3 tbsp whipped cream
freshly ground white pepper
salt

...Ci son delle
cose che basta
che esistano e
si gode a saperlo...

Ingredients

5 medium-sized firm-cooking potatoes
20 g black truffle, cut into slices approx. 3 cm in diameter
oil for deep-frying

Poulard mousse

160 g cooked breast of poulard (fattened chicken)
80 g pâté de foie gras
30 g butter
3 tbsp brown chicken sauce (see "Stocks and Sauces")
2 cl white port
salt
cayenne pepper
150 ml single cream
200 ml whipped cream

Truffled potato crisps with poulard mousse

Finely blend foie gras, poulard breast and butter in a food processor, and pass through a sieve. Reduce chicken sauce somewhat, add single cream and allow to simmer for a further 5 minutes. Slowly stir sauce into mousse. Season to taste with cayenne pepper and a little salt, and carefully fold in whipped cream. Chill for at least 3 hours in a refrigerator.

Peel potatoes and cut lengthways into wafer-thin slices. Place a slice of truffle on each potato slice. Cover with a second potato slice, firmly pressing down at the edges with your fingers, and deep-fry in a chip pan at 160 °C until crisp and golden. Remove crisps from oil, place on absorbent kitchen paper and salt lightly. Place a pointed mound of poulard mousse in the centre of a plate and stick truffle crisps into the side of it. Ill. pp. 96–97.

Serves 4

Baked sauté potatoes with eggs and white truffle

Ingredients
600 g firm (salad) potatoes
(e.g. Siglinde),
boiled in their jackets
6 very fresh eggs
100 g fontina
(Italian cheese from Aosta Valley)
salt
cracked black pepper
1 tbsp oil for frying
30 g butter
60 g white truffle

Peel potatoes and cut into slices 1 cm thick. Fry in a cast-iron pan until crisp, and season. Using an ovenproof dish, build up alternate layers of potato, grated fontina and two fresh eggs. Repeat twice more so that the topmost layer is egg. Sprinkle with cracked black pepper and bake for about 10 minutes in oven preheated to 210 °C. The egg yokes should still be slightly runny. Generously slice white truffle over the potato, and serve in the oven dish.

A very simple recipe, which relies on the eggs being very fresh and being cooked just right. Use plenty of truffle with this dish.

Serves 4

Gratinéd mashed potato with fried egg and white truffle

Peel potatoes, cut in half and boil in salted water until soft. Drain and allow to steam. Pass through a potato press, and with a wooden spoon mash 150 g butter into potato. Gradually add hot milk, season with salt and nutmeg, and spread out flat on four plates.

De-rind boscaiola and cut into small pieces. Sprinkle the pieces plus a few nuts of butter over the mashed potato and allow to melt in oven. Individually fry eggs, seasoning yokes with pepper and whites with a little salt. Place on gratinéd mashed potato and slice truffle over eggs.

Serves 4

Ingredients
700 g floury potatoes
220 g butter
250–350 ml hot milk (depending on consistency of potatoes)
salt
black pepper
freshly grated nutmeg
4 fresh farm eggs
60 g ripe boscaiola
(Italian cheese)
50 g white truffle

Spinach & potato lasagne with white truffle

Pass boiled potatoes through a press while still warm, and work into a consistent dough with egg yokes, flour, semolina and salt. Roll out to a thickness of about 3 mm and cut into eight squares measuring 10 x 10 cm.

Wash the leaf spinach, briefly blanch, refresh, and thoroughly drain. Sweat finely chopped garlic and shallots in butter, and add spinach. Season and pour in double cream. Allow to reduce somewhat, and spread a spoonful over the first square of dough. Repeat, building up layers of potato dough and spinach, topping off with spinach. Sprinkle with grated Parmesan and bake in oven at 190 °C for about 15 minutes. Using a broad spatula, serve on to plates and slice white truffle on top. When the potato comes from the oven, it should be golden at the edges.

Serves 6

Ingredients
900 g floury potatoes, boiled
150 g plain flour – 405 type
100 g semolina
3 egg yokes
salt
300 g leaf spinach
30 g butter
30 g shallots, finely chopped
1/2 tsp garlic, finely chopped
salt
white pepper
freshly grated nutmeg
100 ml double cream
sliced white truffle

Brûlé – the quest for "burnt" earth

In a perfect world, a man would put the tagliatelle on to cook and go off into the woods. There he would immediately find an oak, around the base of which there would be a ring of earth with nothing growing on it – a "brûlé", as it is known. Following a hunch, he would feel around in this soil and unearth 400g of truffle. Meanwhile the noodles would be ready, over which he would slice his precious find. Unfortunately, the world, such as it is, allows the good man to find everything – except a brûlé. Illustrations in books show numerous photogenic, promising-looking earth rings, but this hardly coincides with reality.

Truffles have a habit of defending their habitat against other plants. How this happens no-one knows for sure. But because of this habit and because the mycorrhiza grows symbiotically with a tree's roots, the circular patch of earth forms around the base of the trunk. On the other hand, there are many plants that the truffle does tolerate or which it even benefits from. Examples include the stonecrop, the vine, the dog rose and lavender. Anyone who can "read" the

ground comes well-armed to the hunt for truffles. Such a person can already tell from the vegetation whether the search is worthwhile. Unfortunately, there are other fungi that cause rings around trees. And so all the clues fit – but there's no truffle. But that's the way of the world. It's just not fair.

Grow your own truffle?

Over the ages there have been numerous attempts to cultivate truffles. But only in this century have they met with any success. What we are talking about here is providing the truffle with optimal growing conditions. These are a 10–30 cm layer of nutrient-rich humus overlaying a thick chalk base, broken-up soil, sun, warmth, a southern aspect, and no other fungi such as "Tuber brumale" or the like. In this environment you plant "pre-mycorrhized" saplings (i.e. young trees already "vaccinated" with truffles), cautiously loosen the earth, remove vegetation that might either be harmful or compete for food, and hope that the whole venture will pay off. After a minimum of four or five years, and frequently only after eight, you, the grower, can harvest the first tubers – God willing, and if wild boars have not already scoffed the lot.

Pasta, crespelle, risottos

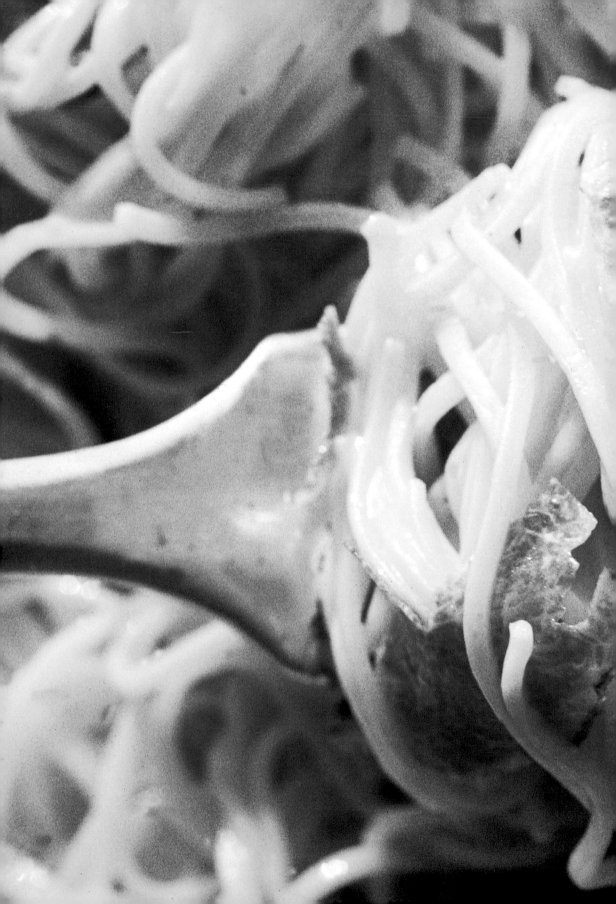

Tagliolini
with white truffle

Roll out pasta dough to desired thickness and cut into sheets 20 cm wide. Allow to dry for a while. Cut into tagliolini (narrow ribbon noodles) and divide into small piles. Bring plenty of salted water to the boil in a large saucepan, and add olive oil and noodles. Briefly bring back to boil and immediately drain off water, but leaving a small amount in saucepan. Add butter, season with nutmeg, and toss together. The residual liquid binds with the butter to make the pasta succulent. Serve at once, lavishly garnishing tagliolini with sliced white truffle. Ill. pp. 110–111.

Serves 4

Ingredients
400 g pasta dough
2 tbsp olive oil
50 g fresh farmhouse butter
freshly grated nutmeg
40–120 g white truffle

Tagliatelle with pumpkin sauce and fresh almonds

Dice pumpkin flesh and braise in butter and chicken stock until pumpkin disintegrates. Season with salt, pepper, white truffle oil and marzipan. Add cream and lightly liquidize.
Cook tagliatelle, drain, mix with a knob of butter, and serve on a dish. Pour pumpkin sauce over tagliatelle, and sprinkle with toasted almond flakes and sliced white truffle.

Serves 4

Ingredients
400 g home-made tagliatelle

Sauce
500 g pumpkin
60 g butter
300 ml chicken stock
(see "Stocks and Sauces")
150 ml single cream
20 g marzipan
70 g flaked almonds, toasted
a few drops of white truffle oil
salt
black pepper
50–60 g white truffle

... di rivedere
le donne grattugiare
impastare, lavorire,
scoperchiare e al
fuoco e mi tornava
in bocca quel
sapore ...

Polenta alla Raffaella

Bring milk and water to boil, stir in maize semolina, adding salt. Stir continually so that polenta does not go lumpy or catch. Simmer gently for about 30 minutes and stir in grated Parmesan and cold butter.

Meanwhile rapidly fry aubergine slices and seppioline in hot olive oil. Season, drain off oil, and continue frying in fresh butter. Serve on a separate dish to the polenta, garnishing only the seppioline with truffle. Especially interesting is the contrasting tastes of truffled seppioline and polenta with aubergines. Ill. p. 117.

Serves 4

Ingredients
75 g maize semolina
250 ml milk
250 ml water
50 g freshly grated Parmesan
40 g butter
salt

also:
300 g seppioline (small squid)
2 tbsp olive oil for frying
20 g butter
2 aubergines, cored and sliced
40 g white truffle

Watercress risotto
with fried frogs' legs
and white truffle

Sweat finely diced shallot and garlic in oil-butter mixture. Add rice and allow to become translucent. Pour in white wine and cook until wine has been absorbed. Gradually add enough hot chicken stock to cover rice. Cook rice for about 15–17 minutes. Ten minutes before rice is ready, mix in coarsely chopped watercress leaves. Season with white pepper and freshly grated nutmeg. Finally, toss with freshly grated Parmesan and ice-cold knobs of butter.

Season frogs' legs with salt and coat with flour. Sear in olive oil, shake off oil, and finish frying in butter. Add to finished risotto and garnish with watercress leaves and sliced white truffle. Ill. p. 121.

Serves 4

Ingredients
30 g extra virgin olive oil
30 g butter
200 g Vialone or other risotto rice
150 ml dry white wine
60 g shallots, finely diced
1/2 tsp garlic, finely chopped
200 g watercress leaves,
coarsely scissored
approx. 600 ml chicken stock
(see "Stocks and Sauces")
80 g young, freshly grated Parmesan
30 g knobs of ice-cold butter
freshly ground white pepper
freshly grated nutmeg
24 frogs' legs (separated from body)
salt
flour for dusting
2 tbsp oil for frying
40 g butter
fresh watercress leaves for
garnishing
40 g white truffle

This is a dish made only in Italy
and France.

Ravioli with sweetbread filling in creamy black truffle sauce

Sweat finely diced vegetables in half the butter, add a little water and braise until soft. Break sweetbreads into small pieces and slightly brown in remaining butter. Season with salt and pepper, and fry slowly for a further 5 minutes. Allow to cool a little and chop small. Add to braised vegetables, pour in cream and simmer until mixture becomes sticky. Season mixture well and mix in chopped parsley. Allow to cool for further preparation.

To make the sauce, melt butter, sweat truffle slices in it, and pour in port and champagne. Reduce, add chicken stock, and again reduce until almost all the liquid has evaporated. Add cream and crème fraîche, adjust seasoning and purée with a hand blender – the black truffle gives the sauce a nice dark colour.

To make ravioli dough, mix flour, eggs, salt, oil and about 60 ml water, and work into a smooth dough. If the dough is too thick, add water a bit at a time, working it in. Cover dough and leave to stand for an hour.

With a pasta machine roll out ravioli dough very thin, brush with egg white, and place small dollops of filling on it at 5-cm intervals. Cover with remaining ravioli dough, press down with the side of the hand, and with a pastry wheel cut out ravioli shapes.

Cook ravioli in plenty of boiling salted water briefly, for about 2 minutes. Remove, toss in a little melted butter, and serve with creamy black truffle sauce.

Serves 8

Cannelloni with walnut filling and white truffle

Lightly fry grated walnut in butter. Combine with egg yokes and mix with robiola. Season with salt, white pepper and freshly grated nutmeg. Spread on freshly made pasta sheets rolled wafer-thin. Roll up the sheets into cannelloni. Layer in a buttered ovenproof dish and pour cream over it. Bake cannelloni in oven for about 15 minutes at 180 °C.

Meanwhile slice artichoke hearts and gently fry in olive oil together with garlic and sprigs of thyme. Place cannelloni on plate, spoon artichoke over pasta, and serve with freshly sliced white truffle.

Serves 4

Ingredients
20 rolled-out sheets of pasta dough, measuring 10 x 10 cm (see recipe on p. 122)
300 g robiola (Italian curd cheese)
2 egg yokes
120 g grated walnuts
20 g butter
120 ml cream
salt
white pepper
freshly grated nutmeg

Cannelloni filling
4 artichoke hearts, cleaned
2 sprigs of thyme
30 ml olive oil
1 unpeeled clove of garlic, crushed
50 g white truffle

Ingredients

30 g extra virgin olive oil
30 g butter
200 g Vialone or other risotto rice
150 ml dry white wine
60 g shallots, finely diced
1/2 tsp finely chopped garlic
200 g root spinach (young
spinach with roots), blanched
and finely chopped
approx. 600 ml chicken stock
(see "Stocks and Sauces")
80 g young Parmesan, freshly
grated
30 g nuts of butter, ice-cold
freshly ground white pepper
freshly grated nutmeg
2 tbsp whipped cream

Garnish

150 g raw calves' sweetbreads,
broken into small pieces
1 tbsp oil for frying
30 g butter
80 g white truffle

Spinach risotto with sweetbreads and white truffle

Sweat finely diced shallot and garlic in oil-butter mixture. Add rice and allow to become translucent. Pour in white wine and reduce. Gradually add enough hot chicken stock to cover rice. Cook rice for about 15–17 minutes. After about five minutes, mix in finely chopped root spinach and season with white pepper and freshly grated nutmeg. Finally, toss rice with freshly grated Parmesan, nuts of ice-cold butter and whipped cream.

Using a non-stick pan, heat oil and butter, fry sweetbreads until golden, and add a little veal sauce. Spoon over risotto and serve with freshly sliced white truffle.

Serves 4

Cardoon crespelle frittered in egg with white truffle

Sweat shallot in butter and add cleaned sliced cardoon. Pour in chicken stock, cover and braise until soft. Add double cream, and season with lemon juice, salt and pepper. Liquidize and strain through a sieve. Spread cardoon purée on crespelle and roll up. Whisk eggs, dip crespelle in egg, and fry in clarified butter on all sides until golden. Cook cardoon strips in veal sauce, and use to cover crespelle on plate. Garnish with freshly sliced white truffle. Ill p. 115.

Serves 4

Ingredients
4 crespelle (crispy pancakes) –
20 cm in diameter
2 eggs
50 g clarified butter

Filling
200 g cardoon, cleaned and sliced
1 tbsp finely chopped shallot
20 g butter
1/4 l light chicken stock
(see "Stocks and Sauces")
75 ml double cream
salt
freshly ground white pepper
a little lemon juice

Garnish
100 g cardoon in strips 5 cm long
15 g butter
100 ml brown veal sauce
(see "Stocks and Sauces")
white pepper
40 g white truffle

Fish, crustaceans and shellfish

Sea trout stuffed with truffle and baked in salt

Ingredients
1 sea trout 1.8 – 2 kg in weight
3 kg unrefined sea salt
3 egg whites
2 heads of celery
10 white peppercorns
300 g white celery sticks
celery leaves for garnishing
40 g black truffle, sliced

Champagne sauce
30 g shallot, finely chopped
40 g white champignons
20 g butter
200 ml champagne
5 cl Noilly Prat
400 ml fish stock
(see "Stocks and Sauces")
250 g cream
150 g crème fraîche
juice of half a lemon
cayenne pepper

Thoroughly clean sea trout inside and out, removing gills. Starting at the dorsal fin, carefully detach skin with a sharp knife. Insert 40 g of sliced truffle and cover over again with skin. Stuff sea trout with crushed peppercorns and celery. Mix sea salt and egg white. Line a baking tray with aluminium foil. Spread part of salt mixture – rather larger than the fish – on tray and lay sea trout on it. Cover with remaining salt mixture, pressing down well to form a fish shape. Bake for 40 minutes in oven preheated to 230 °C.

Meanwhile sweat shallot and champignons in butter. Add champagne and Noilly Prat, and reduce completely. Pour in fish stock and likewise reduce completely. Add crème fraîche and cream, and bring to boil. Season with lemon juice and cayenne pepper, liquidize and sieve. Cut white celery sticks diagonally into pieces 2 cm thick. Braise in a little fish stock, shake off liquid and transfer to fish sauce. Heat remaining truffle slices in fish sauce and serve. Break open salt crust from fish and discard. Remove skin from fish, place fillets on celery sauce, arrange truffle slices around fish, and garnish with celery leaves. Mashed or boiled potatoes make an ideal accompaniment to this dish. Ill. pp. 130–131.

Serves 6

Turbot on mashed potato with veal sauce

Wash fish fillet and dry thoroughly. Criss-cross white skin side with a sharp knife, and cut fillet into four portions. Using a non-stick pan, heat oil and butter until they begin to foam, and place seasoned fillets skin-side down in pan. Basting constantly, fry slowly until golden, but not allowing whey in butter to go brown.

Cook potatoes in plenty of salted water and drain. Push through a potato press and work in chilled butter with a wooden spoon. Pour in enough hot milk to give mashed potato the desired consistency. Season with nutmeg and salt.

Once fried, sprinkle lemon juice over turbot fillet and turn over. Arrange mashed potato flat on a plate and place turbot fillet on it skin side up. Add brown veal sauce to pan juices, and briskly reduce. Dribble a tablespoonful of this sauce over each portion of turbot fillet, and generously grate white truffle over it. One of the finest fish recipes there is!

Serves 4

Ingredients
900 g turbot fillet – if possible, with the white skin side intact, as this gives the fish an almost veal-like taste and can also be eaten
1 tbsp sunflower oil for frying
40 g butter
juice of half a lemon
100 ml brown veal sauce (see "Stocks and Sauces")
60 g white truffle

Mashed potato
500 g floury potatoes, peeled
60 g chilled knobs of butter
150 ml hot milk – add more depending on consistency of potatoes
salt
freshly grated nutmeg

Ingredients

4 crayfish (spiny lobsters, langoustes), 500 g each
60 g butter
salt
30 g oil for frying
50 g black truffle, cut into strips
200 g poivrade – very small artichokes eaten whole and raw
2 tbsp olive oil
freshly ground white pepper

Crayfish fried in butter with black truffle

Place crayfish in boiling water for 10 seconds to kill them. Remove and allow to cool. Cut in half lengthways with a stout knife, and remove stomach and intestinal tract.

Heat oil in a large pan and slowly fry crayfish for about 5 minutes, cut side down. Turn, drain off oil, salt lightly, and add butter. Adjust heat to stop butter burning, and fry for a further 3 to 4 minutes. Shortly before finishing frying, add truffle strips to butter and baste crayfish with it. Wash artichokes, remove green outer leaves and cut off tops. Quarter, and briskly sauté in olive oil. Season, and serve with the fried crayfish. Ill p. 135.

Serves 4

Monkfish with black truffle on lentil sauce

Entirely remove brown skin and veins from monkfish so that only white flesh remains. Peel truffle, cut into slivers 1/2 cm thick, and "lard" fish with them. Season with salt, rapidly sear in oil, and slowly bake for about 20 minutes in an oven pre-heated to 190 °C, basting fish frequently.

Meanwhile fry bacon in oil, slice shallots, garlic and mushrooms, and add to bacon together with thyme. Add tomato purée and balsamic vinegar. Reduce, replenish liquid with chicken stock, and again reduce almost completely. Add cream and crème fraîche, bring back to boil, lightly blend with a hand blender, and sieve. Add green lentils to sauce and season to taste with a pinch of cayenne pepper or balsamic vinegar. Remove baked monkfish from bones, cut into tranches and serve with lentil sauce. Leaf spinach tossed in butter makes a good accompaniment.

Serves 4

Ingredients
1 whole monkfish (angler)
weighing 1200 g
salt
80 g black truffle
20 g butter
3 tbsp olive oil
30 g streaky speck bacon,
smoked
3 shallots
1 clove of garlic
4 champignons
1 tbsp oil
1 sprig of thyme
1/2 tsp tomato purée
4 cl old balsamic vinegar
1/4 l chicken stock
(see "Stocks and Sauces")
200 ml cream
2 tbsp crème fraîche
80 g green mountain lentils,
cooked

Ingredients
2 fresh soles, 600 g each
lemon, cut in half
salt

plus:
2 small firm lettuces
20 g butter
60 g carrot brunoise (finely diced)
60 g black truffle brunoise
salt
400 ml champagne sauce
(see sea trout recipe on page 132)
2 egg yokes for binding

Sole strips on braised lettuce and black truffle

Wash soles, and skin and fillet them, saving bones for fish stock.

Sweat carrot brunoise in butter. Wash lettuce leaves, add to brunoise, season and braise for 5 minutes – uncovered so that the liquid can evaporate.

Mix together 4 tbsp from the champagne sauce with egg yokes. Bring champagne sauce to boil and add this "liaison" to it, being careful not to boil the mixture any more, otherwise egg might curdle. Combine with truffle brunoise, and add this sauce to braised lettuce. Put lettuce and sauce in four buttered cocottes (small ovenproof dishes). Rub sole fillets with lemon halves, season with salt, and fold thin tail ends under. Lay two fillets in each cocotte of lettuce and bake in oven (with grill on) for 4–6 minutes at 220 °C. Ill. pp. 138/139.

Serves 4

Sautéd frogs' legs with parsley butter

Ingredients
24 pairs frogs' legs
salt
white pepper
flour for dusting
3 tbsp olive oil for frying
50 g white truffle

Parsley butter
50 g fresh butter
1 clove of garlic, finely chopped
juice of half a lemon
1/2 tsp finely grated lemon zest
**1/2 bunch flat-leaf parsley,
finely chopped**

**This dish is made only in Italy
and France.**

Wash and skin frogs' legs, separate individual legs, and lay on a dry cloth.

To make parsley butter, beat butter until frothy and fold in parsley, garlic, lemon zest, lemon juice, salt and white pepper. Set aside.

Season frogs' legs, dust with flour, and fry in oil until golden, tossing occasionally. Drain off oil and complete frying in parsley butter. Arrange on a dish and garnish with freshly sliced truffle. May be served with either a champagne risotto or crisp-fried diced potato.

Serves 4

Ingredients
4 heads of chicory
40 g butter
1 tbsp icing sugar
juice of one lime
salt

plus:
16 scallops in their shells
1 tbsp oil for frying
20 g butter
60 g black truffle, sliced
8 cl white port
30 g chilled knobs of butter
cayenne pepper
salt

Sautéd scallops on chicory and black truffle

Open scallops by sliding a stout knife between the two shells and severing the ligament joining the muscle to the flat shell. Lift off flat shell, remove the scallop and discard everything except the scallop and bright orange coral. Wash thoroughly and reserve.

Wash chicory heads and cut out stem. Cut into strips 3 cm thick, place in foaming butter, sprinkle with icing sugar, and add lime juice. Gently cook, not allowing the mixture to take on any colour. Occasionally add a spoonful of water. Season.

Heat truffle slices in butter, season with salt, and add port. Reduce by a half, and bind with chilled butter. Season with cayenne pepper. Clean scallop shells, and fill with glazed chicory. Briefly sauté scallops in oil, season, place on chicory and dribble with truffle butter. Ill. p. 143.

Serves 4

Sautéd lobster with Jerusalem artichoke and black truffle

Ingredients
2 lobsters ca 800 g each
oil for frying
30 g butter

Garnish
200 g Jerusalem artichoke, peeled
100 g cherry tomatoes, peeled
80 g black truffle, sliced
30 g extra virgin olive oil
20 g butter
100 ml fish stock
(see "Stocks and Sauces")
1 garlic clove, unpeeled
1 tsp shallot, finely chopped
a pinch of sugar
freshly ground white pepper
freshly grated nutmeg
salt

Put lobster heads first into boiling water and boil for 10 seconds. Remove, and allow to cool. Separate lobster tails from bodies, halve the latter lengthways and remove stomach. Cut tailpieces crossways into medallions, not forgetting to pull out the intestinal tract.

Sweat finely chopped shallots and garlic clove in olive oil, add peeled tomatoes, and season with salt, white pepper and a pinch of sugar. Pour in fish stock, and simmer until mixture takes on sauce-like consistency.

Halve Jerusalem artichokes lengthways and cut into thin slices. Gently fry in butter until golden, at the same time seasoning with salt and freshly grated nutmeg.

Brown lobster medallions and halved lobster heads in oil in a large pan, and salt. After 2 minutes drain off oil, turn lobster over and sauté again in fresh butter. Just before serving, add truffle slices and toss together well.

Serves 4

The lost truffle paradise –
a fairy tale

Once upon a time, there was a land that had so many truffles that the oaks were bursting with them. Annual production was 2,000 tons, so the story went, and that was after the wild boars had had their share. Then a king or, rather, emperor came to the throne, answering to the name of Bonaparte. He engaged in a spot of warmongering, and for this penchant needed quantities of strong oak, not least for his frigates. The length and breadth of the empire, people fell to clearing the forests. For waging war was still a favourite pastime of rulers. And then industrialization was just getting into gear. Iron needed heat, the railway sleepers. Until, one fine day, everyone noticed that the woods were not up to much any more. And worse still: truffles had become scarce on the plates of my fine lords and ladies. Whereupon the gluttonous and the wise bethought themselves and began replanting the forests. Following the curse of the phylloxera vine louse, the truffle made itself at home in the vineyards, and all was well. In 1914, production was back up to 914 tons. But then came the war to end all wars. And another. And then Brussels. And monoculture. And even if the truffle has not died out completely, today it only just clings to life: a measly 60 tons of it in France. A crying shame, that.

Entrées and
vegetable dishes

Cabbage parcels stuffed with ham and bread

Ingredients

1 good savoy cabbage
200 g white onion, sliced
80 slices black truffle
1 tbsp pork dripping
150 ml chicken stock
(see "Stocks and Sauces")
300 g pigs' caul, rinsed

Filling

300 g mixed mince
(part pork, part veal)
80 g onion
1 small clove of garlic
1 tbsp pork dripping
120 g belly of pork, cooked
1/2 tsp dried marjoram
1 bunch flat-leaf parsley
1 bread roll (a day old)
lukewarm milk
1 egg
salt
black pepper

Peel onion and garlic, and slice. Pluck parsley leaves and wash. Trim rind and gristle from belly of pork and cut into chunks. Heat pork dripping, and glaze onion, garlic and belly of pork in it. Remove from heat and shrivel parsley in it. Soak bread roll in lukewarm milk until soft, and squeeze out excess milk. Combine with glazed onion-pork mixture and grind through the fine blade of a mincer. Add egg, mix with pork and veal mince, and season with salt and black pepper. Remove leaves from cabbage, blanch and refresh in iced water. Thoroughly dry on a cloth and cut out stems. Lay a slice of truffle in the middle of each leaf, top with a good tablespoonful of stuffing, and form into small parcels. Place another truffle slice on the parcels, and wrap in pig's caul. Heat pork dripping in a pan and soften sliced onion in it. Add cabbage parcels, packing them close together, and pour in chicken stock. Cover pan with greaseproof paper, place in oven, and casserole for 35–40 minutes at 180 °C. Serve one cabbage parcel per person, spooning casserole juices over it. Ill. pp. 152–153.

Serves 6–8

Baked truffle

Wrap each scrubbed truffle in a slice of belly of pork. Place on generously buttered baking paper, drizzle with cognac, and season with salt. Wrap up, moisten with water, and ideally place in the faintly glowing embers of a fire, heaping embers on top. Bake for 35 minutes. Remove from embers, peel off burnt baking paper, and serve in a napkin. At home, use the oven in place of the embers. Preheat to 210 °C, place wrapped truffles on a baking tray, and bake in oven for about 45 minutes. Serve as described above. This is one of the oldest truffle recipes, which today is prepared by only a few traditionally run, top restaurants.

Serves 4

Ingredients
4 black truffles, each weighing
60 g – scrubbed but not peeled
4 thin slices belly of pork,
unsmoked
old cognac
salt

... On dit, dans
mon pays natal,
que pendant
un bon repas
on n'a pas soif,
mais bien
« l'aim de boire »

Salsify-truffle ragout under a puff pastry dome

Ingredients
250 g salsify
juice of one lemon
salt
80 g black truffle, finely chopped
20 g butter
100 ml chicken stock
(see "Stocks and Sauces")
freshly grated nutmeg
3 tbsp béchamel sauce
(see "Stocks and Sauces")
1 tbsp crème fraîche
300 g ready-made puff pastry
1 egg yoke for brushing

Peel salsify and boil whole for 10 minutes in salted water and lemon juice. Allow to cool in iced water and cut diagonally into thin slices. Heat butter until it foams, sweat truffles in it and add sliced salsify. Pour in chicken stock, cover and simmer for 5 minutes. Add thick béchamel sauce and crème fraîche, and season with nutmeg. Allow ragout to cool and transfer to small heatproof soup bowls (or soufflé moulds/ramekins).

Roll puff pastry to a thickness of 3 mm, and cut out circles to fit over bowls, allowing a 2-cm overlap. Cover bowls with circles, firmly pinching pastry to rim. Brush with egg yoke and bake for about 5 minutes in oven preheated to 220 °C. Reduce heat to 190 °C and bake for another 10 minutes. Pastry must balloon up into a dome and not subside. Take this dish straight from oven to table, so when you break into the pastry dome, you catch the hot, escaping aroma of truffle. Ill. pp. 156–157.

Serves 6

Chicory with almond cream sauce and black truffle

Sweat finely chopped mushrooms and shallot in butter. Add champagne and Noilly Prat, and reduce almost completely. Pour in chicken stock and again reduce almost completely. Add cream, crème fraîche and lightly toasted almond flakes, and bring to the boil. Season with nutmeg and cayenne pepper, lightly liquidize and pass through a fine sieve.

Meanwhile cut black truffle into strips, warm in a little butter and add Madeira. Peel cooked almonds and cut into slivers. Seal 2 chicory at a time in a bag with salt, sugar, lime juice and half the butter, and simmer in boiling water for 25 minutes. Cool bag in iced water, remove contents and slowly pan-fry with remaining butter. Sprinkle with icing sugar and a pinch of salt, and serve on a plate. Dribble with the finished sauce and garnish with braised truffle strips and almond slivers. Take care that the chicory is not too large or bitter. Ill. p. 161.

Serves 4

Ingredients
4 heads of chicory
40 g butter
3 tbsp icing sugar
juice of one lime
salt

Sauce
20 g shallot
30 g white mushrooms
30 g flaked almonds, lightly toasted until golden
20 g butter
8 cl champagne or white wine
6 cl Noilly Prat
350 ml chicken stock (see "Stocks and Sauces")
200 ml single cream
150 ml crème fraîche
salt
a pinch of cayenne pepper
100 g almonds, cooked in milk
100 g Périgord truffle, peeled
10 g butter
2 cl Madeira

Vegetable panaché with chopped black truffle

Wash and top-and-tail mangetouts, and cut in half crossways. Blanch, refresh in iced water, and allow to drain. Remove stringy bits from celery and cut both celery and spring onions crossways into slices 1/2 cm thick. Peel carrots, cutting longer ones in half. Cut off stems from mushrooms and wash thoroughly in water. Glaze carrots and celery in 10 g of butter with a pinch of sugar and salt until crisp-tender. Sweat spring onions in 10 g of butter, season and braise. Fry mushrooms whole in remaining butter until golden.

Mix mangetouts and braised vegetables together and season with chopped truffle. Toss over a hot flame, serve on an oval dish and garnish with scissored chervil leaves. Other vegetables can be used in this recipe, such as romanesco, cocktail onions, broccoli, salsify and chanterelles. The dish goes well with roast fowl.

Serves 4

Boskop apples
with black truffle
baked in butter

Peel and core apples. Cut into slices 2 mm thick. Peel truffles and likewise cut into fine slices. Alternating apple slices and truffle slices (tie them with kitchen thread so they don't fall apart during baking), lay apple and truffle in a small buttered copper casserole, season with salt, icing sugar and nutmeg, and slowly bake in the oven at 180 °C. Continually baste with butter, ensuring apple-truffle slices do not lose their original apple shape. The truffled apple is ready when the buttery liquid formed during baking takes on a syrupy consistency. Arrange apple on plate, spoon casserole juices on top, and – if desired – serve with a small slice of fried duck pâte. Ill. pp. 164/165.

Serves 4

Ingredients
4 medium-sized Boskop apples
4 black truffles, 50 g apiece
40 g butter
pinch of icing sugar
salt
freshly grated nutmeg

Ingredients

500 g French beans
20 g butter
1 shallot, finely diced
250 g sour cream (with at least
30% fat content) or crème fraîche
60 g black truffle, chopped
50 g speck bacon, finely diced
salt
freshly ground white pepper

French beans with sour cream and black truffle

Wash French beans, top and tail, and cut diagonally into strips. Blanch in plenty of salted water and briefly refresh in cold water. Melt butter and sweat finely diced shallot. Add chopped truffle and blanched beans, and toss over a high heat. Season and pour in sour cream or crème fraîche. Reheat and serve, topping bean mixture with crisp-fried diced bacon. This dish can also be made with Kenya beans or broad beans. Mix the beans in the same proportions, and prepare in the same way. The dish makes a delicious accompaniment to roast lamb or veal. Ill. p. 166.

Serves 4

Braised black truffle
with beaten sherry butter

Ingredients
1 large black truffle weighing
150–180 g
15 g fresh butter
2 cl cream sherry
salt
beaten sherry butter
(see "Stocks and Sauces")

Scrub and carefully peel truffle. Melt butter in a small pan and place whole truffle in it. Season with a little salt, add sherry, and cover at once. Gently braise for 15–20 minutes, turning truffle frequently and basting it with its own juices. Serve in a small silver bowl. Cut slices off truffle about 1/2 cm thick, dot with beaten sherry butter, and eat by itself. This dish is the ultimate truffle-tasting experience. Ill. pp. 170–171.

Serves 2

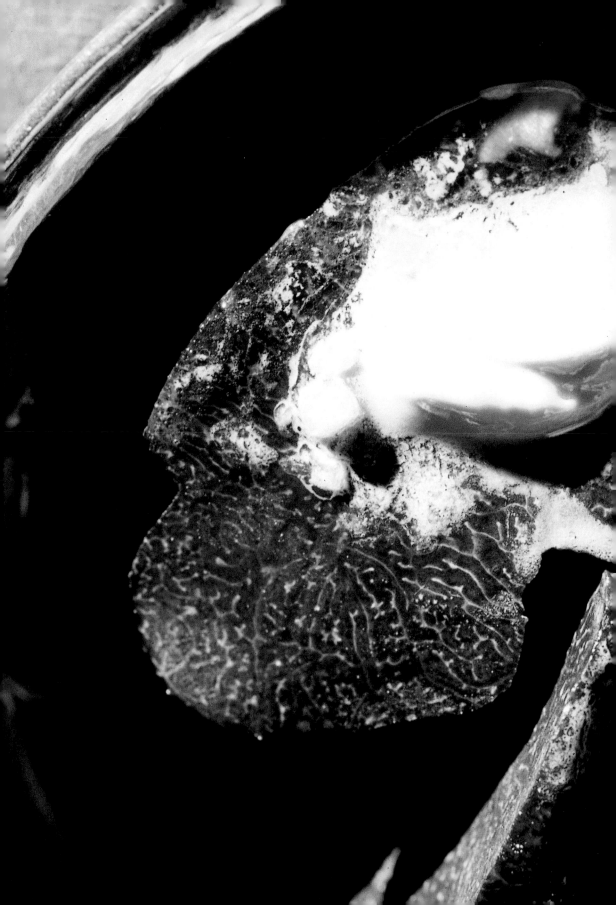

Offal

Fried pâté de foie gras with braised fig

Wash figs and place side by side in a buttered cocotte or small ovenproof dish. Pour in red wine and port, and braise in the oven for about 25–30 minutes at 190 °C. Meanwhile sweat truffle slices in butter and add brown chicken sauce. Gently simmer on a low heat.

Cut foie gras into slices 11/2 cm thick. Season, flour and fry with a little oil on both sides in a non-stick pan. Take one or two figs (depending on how big they are) and garnish with a slice of fried foie gras. Dribble with truffle sauce and serve piping hot. To round off the flavour of the sauce, stir into it a tablespoonful of the fried foie gras pan juices. Ill. p. 174.

Serves 4

Ingredients
8 ripe figs
100 ml full-bodied red wine
(e.g. Merlot)
180 ml port (red)
10 g butter

plus:
350 g pâté de foie gras
salt
freshly ground black pepper
flour for dusting
1 tbsp oil for frying
100 g sliced black truffle
10 g butter
150 ml brown chicken sauce
(see "Stocks and Sauces")

"Foie de veau à la Boulangère"
Slices of calves' liver with glazed shallots and Périgord truffle sauce

Roast shallots in their skins in a cast-iron pan in the oven at 200 °C for about 25 minutes. Peel and reserve. Meanwhile, sweat truffle slices in butter, and pour in brown veal sauce. Slowly simmer over a low flame. Rapidly fry liver slices on both sides in foaming butter. Add cooked shallots, season with salt, black pepper and marjoram, and serve. If this dish is to be eaten as a main course, accompany with mashed potato. Ill. pp. 178–179.

Serves 4

Ingredients
400 g suckling calves' liver, sliced
30 g butter for frying
salt
freshly ground black pepper
a pinch of dried marjoram

plus:
200 g small shallots in their skins
100 g sliced black truffle
10 g butter
150 ml brown veal sauce
(see "Stocks and Sauces")

Foie de veau à la Boulangère

Ingredients

400 g calves' sweetbreads, rinsed
40 g black truffle, slivered
30 g butter
1 tbsp oil for frying
salt
freshly ground white pepper

plus:

80 ml brown veal sauce
(see "Stocks and Sauces")
500 g Jerusalem artichokes
40 g butter
salt
freshly grated nutmeg

Calves' sweetbreads with Jerusalem artichoke and black truffle

Divide calves' sweetbreads into 12 pieces and "lard" them with truffle slivers. Slowly fry on both sides in oil-butter mixture, and season with salt and white pepper. Peel Jerusalem artichokes and cut into thin slices. Fry raw in butter like sauté potatoes. Season with salt and freshly grated nutmeg. Assemble Jerusalem artichoke slices on plates, and arrange fried sweetbreads around them. Add brown veal sauce to sweetbread juices in pan and briefly reduce. Pour over sweetbreads. Garnish with a few celery leaves if desired. Ill. p. 180.

Serves 4

Sautéd calves' sweetbreads with cauliflower beignets and white truffle

Mix white wine, flour, baking powder and egg yokes to a smooth batter, and stir in sunflower oil. Whisk egg whites semi-stiff with a little salt, and carefully fold into batter mixture. Cover and leave to rest for about half an hour.

Rinse calves' sweetbreads, remove membranes and break into walnut-sized pieces. Fry in oil-butter mixture, and season with salt and pepper. Meanwhile, thoroughly dry blanched cauliflower florets, dip in batter and deep-fry at 160 °C. Drain on absorbent kitchen paper. Arrange cauliflower beignets decoratively in middle of the plate, intersperse with fried sweetbreads, garnish with a garland of thick sour cream, and slice white truffle on top.

Serves 4

Ingredients
350 g calves' sweetbreads, rinsed
30 g butter
1 tbsp oil for frying
salt
freshly ground white pepper

plus:
100 ml thick sour cream
200 g small cauliflower florets, blanched
40 g white truffle

Batter
125 g plain flour – 405 type
120 ml dry white wine
40 ml sunflower oil
2 egg yokes
2 eggs
salt
a pinch of baking powder
oil for deep frying

The truffle –
follow your nose

So there the truffle nestles in the chalky humus, feasting on the carbohydrates of its genial host tree, soaking up the warm moisture of the latest thunderstorm and developing a terrific savour – and not a single pig has noticed it?

Not true, unfortunately. As was said at the beginning, pigs are only too capable of sniffing the truffle out. Dogs too, which now easily out-number the pigs. These days, it is only in a few Gallic provinces that pigs are still used for "hunting". There are regular doggy academies, where the animals learn to track down the truffly prey. A full £1000 is said to be the cost of such a training, and it is not even tax-deductible. A third animal that cannot resist the "erotic" lure of the truffle is the goat. But only in Italy, and there only in Sardinia. Harvesting is done mostly at night. The advantages are obvious: no taxman, no rivals, no distractions for the dogs.

The quirkiest method of hunting requires having a good eye.

You lie down on the ground, hoping to catch sight of a fly of the genus "Suillia". This fly likes to pamper its eggs with truffle aroma. Accordingly, it lays them directly above the source of that aroma. If only life were so simple ...

PLATS D

Coq au l

Langue sa

Lapin à la

JOUR
'HUI.

Piquante

outarde

Poultry dishes

Roast wild duck stuffed with fig and truffle

To make stuffing, cut baguette into thin slices and moisten with milk. Beat eggs with a fork and add. Coarsely dice duck liver and truffle, quarter marinated figs, carefully mix together, and adjust seasoning. Gut and wash wild ducks, and stuff with the mixture. Sew together belly opening with kitchen thread, and rub plenty of salt into skin.

Heat clarified butter in a suitable roasting tray, add juniper berries and bay leaves, and place ducks in tray on their legs. Preheat oven to 190 °C, and roast on all sides for about 20 minutes, basting frequently. Turn birds on their backs and roast for another 20 minutes. By now skin on breast should be nice and crisp. Increase temperature if necessary.

Wash autumn chanterelles, sort and drain thoroughly. Make nut butter in a large pan and add mushrooms. Sauté, season, and add finely diced shallot and chopped parsley. Assemble on plate and lay roast wild duck on top, not forgetting to remove kitchen thread! Serve with chicken sauce, using stuffing as garnish. Ill. pp. 192–193.

Serves 4

Ingredients
2 wild ducks weighing 800 g each
salt
white pepper
5 juniper berries
3 bay leaves
40 g clarified butter
300 g fresh autumn chanterelles
30 g butter
20 g shallot, finely chopped
1 tsp flat-leaf parsley, chopped

Stuffing
80 g baguette (French stick)
2 eggs
50 ml full-cream milk
60 g duck liver
150 g dried figs, marinated in port
80 g black truffle
salt
freshly ground black pepper
freshly grated nutmeg

Breast of pheasant on sauerkraut with black truffle sauce and mashed potato

Lightly caramelize sugar in a pan, add vinegar and reduce. Add goose dripping and soften sliced onion until translucent. Add sauerkraut, bouquet garni and belly of pork. Pour in apple juice and water, cover pan, and place in oven preheated to 190 °C for half an hour. Take out bouquet garni and pork belly. If necessary, bind with a little cornflour and add peeled white grapes.

Season pheasant breasts and fry skin side down with juniper berries, basting frequently.

Meanwhile, sweat truffle slices in butter, and add brown chicken sauce. Simmer gently. Place sauerkraut in middle of plate, lay pheasant breast on top (skin side up), and spoon truffle sauce all around. Serve mashed potato (see recipe on p. 102) separately.

Serves 4

see recipe on p. 102

Ingredients
4 pheasant breasts
with skin and wings
30 g clarified butter
4 juniper berries
100 g black truffle, sliced
10 g butter
150 ml brown chicken sauce
(see "Stocks and Sauces")

Sauerkraut
400 g sauerkraut from the barrel
2 tbsp sugar
4 tbsp cider vinegar
2 tbsp goose dripping
2 onions, sliced
1/8 l apple juice
1/8 l water
100 g belly of pork, in one piece
150 g white grapes, skinned and seeded

Bouquet garni
1 tsp caraway
10 juniper berries
3 cloves
10 white peppercorns
1 bay leaf
1 clove of garlic

Poulard demi-deuil

Ingredients
**1 poulard (fattened chicken)
weighing 1.8–2.2 kg
100 g white truffle, sliced
80 g clarified butter
5 l chicken stock
(see "Stocks and Sauces")
200 g shallots, unpeeled
3 bay leaves
200 ml creamy truffle sauce
(see "Stocks and Sauces")**

Gut and clean poulard. Using fingers, detach bird's skin from flesh, starting at the neck. Working carefully, loosen skin from breast and legs. Insert truffle slices under skin, ensuring even distribution, and truss with kitchen string.

Traditionally, after trussing, poulard in "half mourning" used to be wrapped in a cloth and buried for 3 days. This enabled the truffle flavours to unfold, while the soil added a certain earthy touch. To achieve a similar effect, the bird can be wrapped for 24 hours in a cloth soaked with vinegar, which causes a slight maturation process. Heat chicken stock until gently simmering, add poulard together with shallots and bay leaves, and poach for a good half hour. Remove and allow to drain. Season with a little salt and roast in oven for another hour in clarified butter at 160 °C, not forgetting to lay the fowl first on its legs. Baste frequently. Remove from oven, carve and serve with creamy truffle sauce (see recipe on p. 244). Pilau rice makes a good accompaniment. Ill. p. 197.

Serves 6–8

Roast cockerel
with chestnuts

Gut, wash and thoroughly dry cockerel. Season with salt and pepper inside and out. Stuff with celery, whole shallots, parsley stalks and bay leaves. Truss bird with kitchen string so that it keeps its shape during roasting. Heat oil in a suitable roasting tray, and place cockerel in it resting on its legs. Preheat oven to 190 °C and roast bird for about 20 minutes on all sides, basting frequently. Then turn on its back and roast for another 20 minutes. By now, skin on breast should be nice and crisp. Increase temperature if necessary.

Sweat peeled chestnuts in butter in a pan, season with salt and add apple juice. Cover and braise for a good 10 minutes. Take roast cockerel out of tray and keep warm. Skim off fat from tray, and add a little water to the roasting juices. Add braised chestnuts and chicken sauce, briefly reheat, and place bird on chestnuts. Carve cockerel and assemble on plate by placing meat on chestnuts and sauce. Slice white truffle over the cockerel meat. Ill. pp. 200–201.

Serves 6

Ingredients
1 cockerel weighing approx. 1.8 kg
1 head of celery
3 shallots, whole
a few parsley stalks
2 bay leaves
salt
freshly ground white pepper
oil for frying
320 g chestnuts, peeled
15 g butter
150 ml clear apple juice
salt
100 ml brown chicken sauce
(see "Stocks and Sauces")
40 g white truffle

Stuffed quails with prunes and black truffle

Gut, wash and dry quails. Season with salt and pepper, and stuff with prunes marinated in Armagnac. Place in a suitable roasting tray together with rosemary and bay leaves. Roast in oven for 20 minutes at 210 °C or until the skin is nice and crispy.

Remove almost cooked quails from roasting tray. Cut baguette into slices 1 cm thick and lay these flat on bottom of tray. Layer truffle slices on bread, and replace quails on top. Spoon over chicken sauce and return to oven for a further 5 minutes to glaze. The baguette slices should have soaked up the sauce. A young (ruby) port goes well with this dish, the port complementing the sweetness of the prunes. Ill. p. 203.

Serves 6

Ingredients
6 nice plump quails
200 g prunes
4 cl old Armagnac
1 sprig of rosemary
4 bay leaves
2 cloves
30 g butter
salt
white pepper
1/2 baguette (French stick)
100 g black truffle, sliced
150 ml brown chicken sauce
(see "Stocks and Sauces")

Home-smoked breast of duck on turnip and truffle sauce

Trim duck breasts, removing any fat or veins. Score skin with crisscross lines. Using a mortar, pound together spices with salt and sugar, and rub into duck breasts. Thread a piece of string through the flatter side of the duck breasts, and hang them for 3 days in a fireplace by an open fire. Coarsely grate turnips. Soften shallots in duck dripping until translucent. Add honey, cider vinegar and turnips, season and pour in chicken stock. Cover and simmer for about an hour on a low heat. To make truffle sauce, gently soften truffle slices in butter, add Madeira and reduce. Pour in chicken sauce and simmer very gently for a further 10 minutes. Arrange turnip on an oval dish. Thinly slice smoked duck breast and lay on turnip with slices overlapping. Pour truffle sauce all around and serve with mashed potato. Ill. pp. 206/207.

Serves 4

Ingredients
2 fresh duck breasts
1 tbsp salt
1/2 tbsp sugar
1/2 tsp white pepper
1/2 tsp coriander seeds
3 juniper berries
3 allspice berries
500 g turnips
80 g shallots, sliced
50 g duck dripping
1 tbsp honey
2 tbsp cider vinegar
2 tbsp light chicken stock
(see "Stocks and Sauces")
salt
white pepper
80 g black truffle, sliced
20 g butter
4 cl Madeira
150 ml chicken sauce
(see "Stocks and Sauces")

Truffles and wine – a kind of love-hate relationship

The strictly results-oriented gourmet will not be long detained by this subject. After all, the two hardly make the perfect couple on the palate. The reason why we take up the theme lies in the, let's say, "ticklish relationship" between these two pleasures. Truffles and wine share the same climatic zones. They like warmth and a southerly aspect, and only tolerate frost in homeopathic doses. The making of a great wine is a soil not too rich in humus, but rather on the barren side, and with an abundance of minerals – i.e. chalk, which the truffle also likes. If we consider the matter closely, we see that the truffle owes wine a kind of debt. Only too happily does it ensconce itself among old vines, especially if an oak has also found its way there. In times gone by, there was almost exclusively mixed cultivation, with vines, for example, growing alongside trees. So this favourable constellation arose inevitably. Hence the vineyard name "La Truffière" at the wine estate Cassagne Haut-Canon in Fronsac, where the owner likes to talk about the truffles that even today he still finds in the vineyard between the oaks.

Why the truffle seeks the company of old vines is explained by the fact that the roots make a grand job of preparing the soil.

They loosen it, break up the sometimes compact chalk, and stand with the truffle in a reciprocal relationship that is still not fully understood. However, today the liaison is something of a rarity because on the one hand mixed cultivation has almost died out, and on the other all the old vines are ripped out whenever a vineyard is replanted. In the last third of the previous century, by contrast, the truffle could sit down to a hearty meal. The phylloxera vine beetle devastated the vineyards, leaving the truffle with optimally prepared soil. Production rocketed, alleviating the catastrophe for some vintners. So where, you might ask, is the catch in this hunky-dory relationship? It has to do with the weather. Grapes like warm weather, but not too warm, so that the vegetation period is as long as possible and the grapes are not ready too early. And they like relatively dry conditions in August,

September and October. But it is precisely then that the truffle likes hot humid weather. Under these conditions, it grows splendidly – as do other harmful fungi that have a detrimental effect on the grape. In addition, rain causes the vine to take up too much water, diluting the concentration of aroma. In short, and as mentioned at the outset:

A good year for truffles means a bad vintage, and vice versa.

Meat dishes

Ingredients
**500 g truffled salsiccia
(Italian sausage)
30 g butter
a few sage leaves**

Mashed potato
**500 g floury potatoes
100 g cold butter
salt
freshly grated nutmeg**

Salsiccia
with mashed potato
and white truffle

Boil potatoes in salted water until soft. Drain and allow to steam. Add butter, season with nutmeg and allow to stand for a minute without mixing. Then, using a potato masher only, rapidly work in the butter. This simple version of mashed potato makes a marvellous foil to truffled salsiccia.

Fry salsiccia slowly in butter and, just before serving, add sage leaves. Slice white truffle on top according to taste and mood. Ill. pp. 216–217.

Serves 4

Boiled ham
with truffle sauce

Ingredients
1 cured ham weighing
ca 2 1/2–3 kg, uncooked
2 onions
4 cloves
2 bay leaves
10 white peppercorns

plus:
truffle sauce – see "Stocks and
Sauces" and recipe for Filet
Rossini on p. 224, but chop the
truffles coarsely and triple the
amount of sauce

Get your local butcher to cure the ham (order about one week in advance). Peel onions and "lard" them with bay leaves and cloves.

Fill a suitable pan with water and bring to the boil. Add ham, peppercorns and "larded" onions. Gently simmer ham for 2 to 3 hours. Transfer to a large wooden platter and carve at table. Serve with truffle sauce and mashed potato (see recipe on p.102).

Serves 10–12

Filed Rossini

Filet Rossini

Season fillet steaks with salt and black pepper, and gently fry in oil-butter mixture on both sides. Cooking time depends on how well done the steaks should be – for medium rare (steaks still pink inside), fry for about 8 minutes. Meanwhile sweat sliced truffle in butter, add Madeira and pour in brown veal sauce. Simmer on a low heat.

Lightly toast bread and place in centre of plate. Place fillet steaks on bread and keep warm in oven. Season slices of foie gras, dust with flour, and briefly fry in a non-stick pan. Lay these foie gras slices on the tournedos steaks and immediately dribble with truffle sauce. Ill. p. 220.

Serves 4

Ingredients
4 x 140 g tournedos steaks
10 g butter
2 tbsp oil for frying

plus
150 g pâté de foie gras cut into 4 slices
salt
freshly ground black pepper
flour for dusting
4 slices of tin loaf bread 1 cm thick, with crusts removed

Truffle sauce
120 g black truffle, sliced
20 g butter
4 cl Madeira
150 ml brown veal sauce (see "Stocks and Sauces")
a few knobs of chilled butter for binding

Rabbit braised in pumpkin sauce

Sweat chopped leek, celeriac and garlic in butter. Add pumpkin cubes, and braise slowly until liquid has almost boiled away. Dust with paprika powder and immediately add a few dashes of cider vinegar, so paprika does not turn bitter. Add crushed allspice berries and pour in chicken stock. Gently simmer for 15 minutes, liquidize and strain through a fine sieve. Season with nutmeg, add cream and set aside.

Joint rabbit into legs, shoulders and two halved back pieces. Season, add rosemary and bay leaves, and braise in butter in the oven for about 30 minutes at 170 °C, not allowing meat to brown. If pan juices become too dry, add some water. Transfer already-made pumpkin sauce to rabbit, cover and return to oven for a further 10 minutes. Serve with potato gnocchi or runny polenta, and sprinkle with sliced white truffle. Ill. p. 223.

Serves 6

Ingredients
1 meaty rabbit weighing about 1.8 kg
1 sprig rosemary
2 bay leaves
30 g butter
salt
freshly ground white pepper

Pumpkin sauce
250 g pumpkin, coarsely diced
60 g leek, white part only
60 g celeriac
1/2 clove garlic
30 g butter
1 tsp sweet paprika powder
2 allspice berries, crushed
a few dashes of cider vinegar
3/4 l chicken stock
(see "Stocks and Sauces")
75 ml cream
salt
freshly grated nutmeg
40 g white truffle

Ingredients
500 g puff pastry
1 egg yoke for brushing

Stuffing
260 g lean lamb, from the leg
50 g smoked belly of pork
50 g sultanas, steeped in cognac
80 g pâté de foie gras,
cut into small cubes
50 g walnuts, coarsely chopped
1 egg
50 ml cream
salt
freshly ground white pepper
8 small black truffles,
each weighing 30 g, peeled
10 g butter
2 cl Madeira

Lamb patties stuffed with black truffle and sultanas

Using a coarse blade, grind lamb and belly of pork through a meat mincer. Combine with sultanas, diced foie gras, walnuts, egg, cream and seasoning to form a consistent mixture. Sweat peeled truffles in butter in a pan, add Madeira, cover and braise for a few minutes. Remove, and add the remaining juices to form the filling.

Roll puff pastry 2 mm thick, and cut out 16 squares measuring 9 x 9 cm. Put 40 g of stuffing on 8 squares, leaving at least 1 cm clear at the edges. Brush edge with egg yoke. Place a truffle in the middle of each, and cover with unused squares. Press edges down well, and brush with egg yoke. Preheat oven to 220 °C and bake patties for 5 minutes, then reduce heat to 180 °C, and bake until pastry is crisp. This dish can also be made using smaller pastry squares, resulting in a tasty snack to serve to guests with an aperitif. Ill. pp. 226/227.

Serves 8

Venison crepinettes with black truffle and stewed apple

Sweat finely chopped mushrooms and celery brunoise in butter, splash in a few dashes of vinegar, and braise until soft. When the liquid has boiled off, transfer to a bowl and allow to cool. Bind with forcemeat and season.

Trim off any fat or gristle from venison, season with salt, pepper and finely ground juniper, and coat all round with forcemeat. Place a slice of truffle on top and bottom, and wrap in pigs' caul.

Melt butter, sweat green peppercorns in it, and add lemon juice. Add sugar and lemon zest, and briefly cook through. Toss baby apples in buttery mixture and remove from heat – they should be served lukewarm.

Slowly fry venison crepinettes for about 4 minutes on both sides in oil, with crushed juniper berries and a little orange peel. Assemble venison crepinettes two a time on oval plates, and garnish with glazed baby apples. Add brown veal sauce to pan juices, sieve and reduce a little. Spoon over crepinettes and serve. Ill. pp. 228–229.

Serves 4

Ingredients

8 venison loin chops (approx. 350 g)
salt
black pepper
1/2 tsp finely ground juniper berries
300 g pigs' caul, rinsed
10 crushed juniper berries
120 ml brown veal sauce (see "Stocks and Sauces")
100 g mushrooms, finely chopped
100 g celery brunoise (finely diced)
10 g butter
a few dashes white wine vinegar
60 g venison forcemeat consisting of:
venison offcuts
pâté de foie gras
port (red)
salt and white pepper
80 g black truffle, sliced
1 glassful of baby apples, marinated
30 g brown sugar
10 g butter
10 g green peppercorns
1 tsp lemon peel, finely chopped
juice of half a lemon
orange peel

... C'est la plus capricieuse, la plus révérée des princesses noires. On la paie son poids d'or ...

Neck of veal with celery and truffle butter

Ingredients
1.2 kg neck of veal in one piece
80 g celeriac,
cut into slivers 1/2 cm thick
salt
a little sugar
freshly ground white pepper
30 g butter
250 g small, tart Boskop apples
4 cl calvados
truffle butter
(see "Stocks and Sauces")

Using a larding needle, "lard" neck of veal with raw celeriac slivers. Shape meat by trussing with kitchen string. Core and quarter apples, but do not peel. Mix apple with a dash of calvados. Season veal and lightly brown in a casserole in butter. Add quartered apples, sprinkle with a little sugar, cover, and braise in oven at 180 °C. From time to time, add a little calvados to pan juices, spooning them over the veal. The joint should be cooked after 1 $^1/_4$ –1 $^1/_2$ hours.

Remove string from veal and carve. Serve with apples, and garnish slices of meat with truffle butter. Good accompaniments to this dish are fresh home-made noodles or small jacket-baked potatoes. Ill. p. 232.

Serves 6–8

Lamb chops in artichoke and truffle crust

Remove outer leaves from artichokes, break off stalks and cut so as to leave only the hearts. Scrape out the choke with a small spoon and discard. Cut hearts into fine slices, lightly bind with truffle strips, salt, egg yoke and flour, and coat lamb chops.

Pour olive oil into a non-stick pan, add thyme and garlic, and fry coated lamb chops on both sides until golden. Remove, add veal sauce to pan juices, strain and spoon around the chops. Serve with sautéd potato gnocchi or polenta.

Serves 4

Ingredients
8 lamb chops weighing approx.
380–400 g in total
salt
freshly ground black pepper
1 sprig of thyme
2 unpeeled cloves of garlic,
crushed
1 tbsp olive oil for frying
140 ml brown veal sauce
(see "Stocks and Sauces")
4 large globe artichokes
50 g black truffle,
cut into fine strips
salt
1 egg yoke
1 tsp flour

Stocks, sauces
and butters

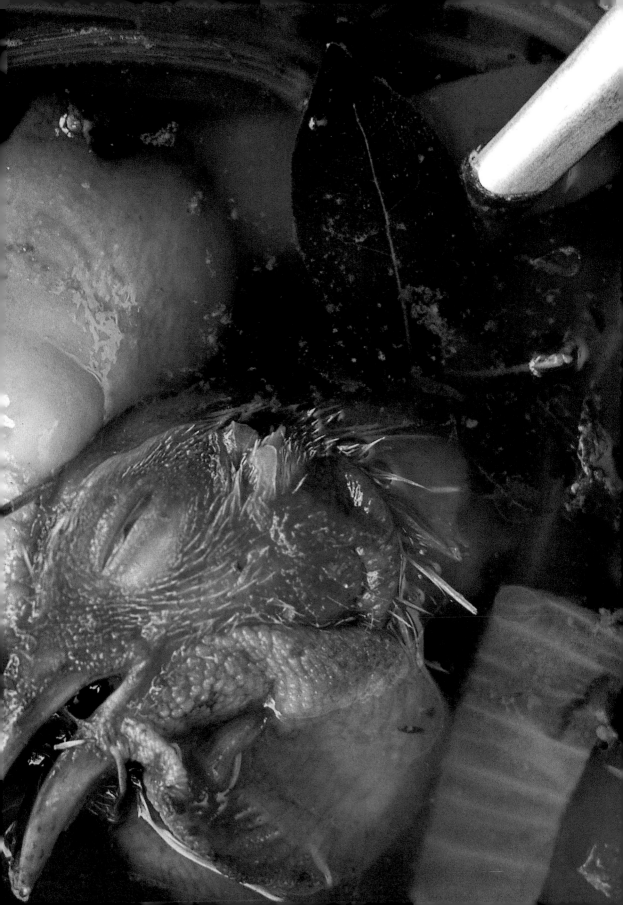

Chicken stock

Ingredients
**1 kg chicken trimmings
(wings, necks, bones etc.)
2 l water
150 g celeriac
150 g celery
220 g onions in their skins
80 g shallots, peeled
1 leek
1 parsley root, peeled
2 cloves of garlic, peeled
3 bay leaves
2 cloves
8 juniper berries
4 allspice berries
10 black peppercorns
1 tbsp coarse salt
a few parsley stalks, if to hand**

Makes 2 litres

Wash chicken trimmings, place in a large stockpot with salt and cold water, and bring to the boil, skimming off any foam. Gently simmer for 1^1/$_2$ hours, not skimming off fat – after straining, the fat serves as a protective film. Add vegetables, spices and herbs, and simmer for a further hour. From time to time add water, to top up stock to its original volume. Strain stock first through a colander and then through a fine sieve, to remove all residue. Cool and then store in refrigerator until required – will keep for at least a week. Ill. pp. 238–239.

Truffle vinaigrette

Ingredients
**80 g black truffle, finely chopped
4 cl port (red)
2 tbsp good-quality balsamic
vinegar
8 tbsp red wine vinegar
5 tbsp extra virgin olive oil
7 tbsp cold-pressed sunflower oil
salt
sugar
freshly ground black pepper**

Makes 8 portions

Sweat finely chopped truffle in 2 tbsp sunflower oil, add port, reduce, and season with salt, sugar and black pepper. Add balsamic vinegar and red wine vinegar, and slowly stir in the two oils. Truffle vinaigrette tastes best after 24 hours and served lukewarm.

Chicken sauce

Chop chicken trimmings small. Peel vegetables and cut into $^1/_2$ cm cubes. First lightly oven-brown chicken trimmings in a large roasting tin. Then add diced vegetables, spices and herbs, and continue browning in the oven at 220 °C. Once vegetables are translucent, add tomato purée and return briefly to oven. Transfer to a large stockpot, add white wine and Madeira, and reduce liquid almost entirely. Pour in water and simmer gently for about 4 hours. Strain sauce through a colander and then a fine sieve. Skim off fat and bind with a little cornflour, if desired. At the end, only 1 litre of liquid should remain.

Ingredients
2 kg chopped chicken trimmings
(wings, necks, bones etc.)
350 g shallots
100 g carrot
150 g celery
80 g mushrooms
2 tbsp oil for frying
1 tbsp tomato purée
5 cloves of garlic
2 bay leaves
1/2 sprig of rosemary
1/2 sprig of thyme
5 cloves
5 allspice berries
10 white peppercorns
1 tsp coarse sea salt
200 ml dry white wine
200 ml Madeira
3 l water
a little cornflour for binding,
if required

Makes 1 litre

Fish stock

Cut fish trimmings into small pieces and wash thoroughly under running water. Remove skin and fins. Dice vegetables into $^1/_2$ cm cubes and sweat in oil. Add well-drained fish trimmings and again lightly sweat. Pour in white wine, add herbs and spices, and fill up with water. Bring to the boil and skim. Add various herb stalks, if available, and allow to infuse for 20 minutes. Strain through muslin, and store in refrigerator for further use.

Ingredients
1 kg turbot and sole fish bones,
including heads
150 g onions, peeled
80 g fennel
120 g celery
2 cloves of garlic
3 bay leaves
1 sprig of thyme
150 ml dry white wine
sea salt
10 white peppercorns
1 l water

Makes 1 litre

Brown veal sauce

Ingredients
2 kg chopped calves' bones
350 g onions
100 g carrots
150 g celery
80 g celeriac
2 tbsp oil for roasting
2 tbsp tomato purée
3 cloves of garlic
3 bay leaves
1 sprig of rosemary
1 sprig of thyme
5 cloves
10 allspice berries
10 white peppercorns
1 tsp coarse sea salt
200 ml dry white wine
200 ml Madeira
3 l water
a little cornflour for binding, if required

Makes 1 litre

Get your butcher to break up bones as finely as possible so that all the marrow is extracted during cooking. Peel vegetables and dice coarsely. First, lightly oven-brown bones in a large roasting tin. Then add vegetables, spices and herbs, and continue browning in oven at 220 °C. When vegetables are translucent, add tomato purée and return briefly to oven. Transfer to a large stockpot, add white wine and Madeira, and reduce almost all the liquid away. Pour in water and simmer gently for about 4 hours. Strain sauce first through a colander and then through a fine sieve. Skim off fat and bind with a little cornflour, if desired. At the end, only 1 litre of liquid should remain.

Creamy Périgord truffle sauce

Ingredients
20 g shallots
30 g white mushrooms
20 g butter
8 cl champagne or white wine
6 cl white port
4 cl Madeira
350 ml chicken stock
(see recipe above)
200 ml single cream
150 ml crème fraîche
salt
freshly grated nutmeg
a pinch of cayenne pepper
100 g Périgord truffle, peeled
10 g butter
2 cl Madeira

Makes 4 portions

Sweat finely sliced mushrooms and shallots in butter. Add champagne, white port and Madeira, and cook until almost completely reduced. Pour in chicken stock and again reduce almost completely. Add cream and crème fraîche, season with nutmeg and cayenne pepper, bring to boil, briefly liquidize, and strain through a fine sieve. Meanwhile thinly slice black truffle and warm in a little butter. Add Madeira and the sauce made earlier. Allow to infuse for 5 minutes, and just before serving add a spoonful of whipped cream, if desired. This sauce goes well with roast or casseroled poultry, filled pasta and lightly cooked veal dishes.

Basic aspic jelly

Put meat and blanched calves' hoofs (which provide the gelatine) in cold water, add a tablespoonful of salt, and bring to the boil. Skim off any foam. Reduce heat, and gently simmer for a further 3 hours. Add vegetables, spices and herbs, and continue to cook for another $3/4$ hour. Remove meat after about 2 hours, and reserve for use in other dishes. Strain liquid through a fine muslin cloth and skim off all fat. Season well, pour into a bowl and allow to cool. Best made a day in advance so the aspic can cool thoroughly. Serve chopped aspic with starters, or use for coating mousses. Ill. p. 242.

Ingredients
1 kg beef (brisket, leg or shin)
400 g calves' hoofs
3 unpeeled onions,
halved and browned
2 cloves of garlic
260 g carrots
150 g celeriac
100 g celery
3 ripe tomatoes
1 parsley root
3 bay leaves
3 sprigs of lovage
parsley stalks
10 black peppercorns
5 allspice berries
freshly grated nutmeg
salt
2 1/2 l water

Makes 2 litres

Truffle slices steeped in Madeira

Ingredients
**1 preserving jar
black truffle, sliced
a good Madeira
pinch of salt**

Lightly salt truffle skins, truffle ends and slices, put into a preserving jar, and add Madeira until almost covered. Use slices when making sauces, vinaigrettes, aspics, fillings and stuffings. In refrigerator will keep for at least a week. Ill. p. 246.

Béchamel sauce

Ingredients
**500 ml milk
60 g butter
60 g plain flour – 405 type
250 ml cream
juice of half a lemon
1 onion "larded" with 2 cloves
and a bay leaf
salt
freshly grated nutmeg**

Makes 10 portions

Lightly fry flour in butter. Pour in cold milk and bring to boil, stirring constantly. Add "larded" onion, and simmer gently for 30 minutes, stirring from time to time. Strain through a fine sieve, stir in cream, and season with salt, nutmeg and lemon juice. Can be used for binding cream soups, instead of cream or crème fraîche, or for binding vegetables or meat croquettes.

Black truffle butter

Beat butter in a bowl until fluffy and white. Sweat chopped truffle in a little butter, add Madeira, reduce until syrupy in consistency, and whisk into the remaining butter. Season with salt and freshly grated nutmeg, and serve at once. Goes well with veal or poultry casseroles, or can be used for whisking into sauces.

Ingredients
250 g fresh unsalted butter
60 g fresh black truffle
(or truffle offcuts),
finely chopped
8 cl Madeira
a pinch of salt
freshly grated nutmeg

Serves 4

Beaten sherry butter

Beat sweet-cream butter in a bowl until white and fluffy. Reduce cream sherry in a pan until syrupy, and then whisk into butter. Season with salt and freshly grated nutmeg, and serve at once. Do not chill butter, as this causes it to lose some of its taste and silky texture. Ill. p. 243.

Ingredients
250 g fresh sweet-cream butter
200 ml cream sherry
a pinch of salt
freshly grated nutmeg

Serves 4

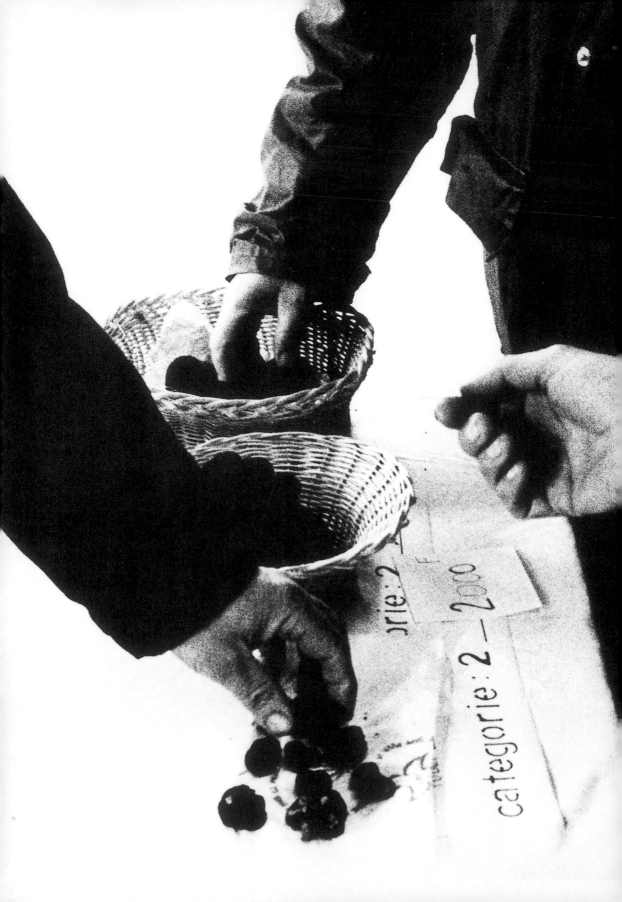

The truffle –
a story of sharp
practices

The "melanosporum" and the "magnatum" are the
most expensive kinds of truffle, and for that reason
the most likely to be faked. The simplest method is
to take cheaper "aestiva" truffles from Italy, Spain
or Yugoslavia and dye them darker. In a trice, you
then have more valuable "melanospora" and a mark-
up of 500%. The "Terfizia leonis", the sand truffle
from North Africa, is tweaked in exactly the same
way. The weight of rather trifling truffles is increased
by rubbing earth into them or by pressing lead
pellets into them. And the "artists" among the
conmen are wizards with toothpicks: they cobble
together small unprepossessing truffles into a first-
rate specimen, rub some earth over it and, hey
presto, you have the best truffle that has ever been
offered for sale in the market.

But the greatest danger comes from China. It is
called "Tuber indicum", and at first glance looks

almost exactly the same as the "melanosporum". Some middlemen exploit the resemblance, because the 'indicum' is some six to eight times cheaper to buy than the "Périgord" truffle. And it's not just that it's offered for sale under a false and more lucrative name. In the eyes of truffle sellers and hunters, it destroys market prices, even when sold legally. Just go to the market in Lalbenque and try to get rid of some "Tuber indicum". Have fun!

Desserts and cheese dishes

Jelly à la Marcela

Heat port and dissolve sugar and softened gelatine in it. Combine tea and rum, add port mixture, pour into glasses and allow to set.

Peel truffle and cut into slices 3 mm thick. Reduce additional port and sugar by three quarters, add truffle slices to the still warm liquid, and allow to cool.

Whip cream and deseeded vanilla pod until semi-stiff. Place dollops on the tea jelly, garnish with macerated truffle strips, and lightly sprinkle with brown sugar. Ill. pp. 256/257.

Ingredients
1/4 l strong black tea
4 cl old rum
30 g brown sugar
2 cl old port (red)
6 g gelatine (3 sheets)

plus
100 g cream
1/4 vanilla pod, split lengthways
and seeds scraped out
50 g black truffle
20 g brown sugar
8 cl old port (red)

Serves 4

Mascarpone ice cream with black truffle

Combine milk and half the sugar, and bring to the boil. Beat egg yokes and remaining sugar until fluffy, and add to milk. Thicken to a custard consistency in a bain-marie. Stir chopped truffle and mascarpone into the hot mixture, and allow to cool. Churn in an ice-cream machine, and store in deep freezer. Garnish scoops of mascarpone ice cream with a few truffle strips and serve.

Serves 4–6

Ingredients
700 ml full-cream milk
10 egg yokes
260 g sugar
90 g black truffle
300 g mascarpone cheese

Chocolate truffles

Ingredients
1/4 l double cream
375 g plain chocolate – 55% cocoa
solids
120 g black truffle, finely chopped
30 g bitter chocolate
140 g bitter chocolate powder
50 g granulated sugar

Makes 35 truffles

Pour double cream into a pan and bring to the boil. Remove from heat and add chopped truffle. Finely grate 350 g of chocolate and pour hot cream-truffle mixture over chocolate. Keep stirring until the mixture is smooth – the "ganache". Cool in refrigerator for 2 hours. Using a piping bag, squeeze out small balls and hand-roll. Return to refrigerator for a few minutes. Grate remaining chocolate into bitter chocolate and melt in a bain-marie. Draw truffles one by one through melted chocolate with a chocolate fork and turn in cocoa powder and granulated sugar. Remove excess cocoa, and store truffles in a cool place – but not in the refrigerator! Ill. pp. 260–261.

Truffled goats' quark baked in filo pastry

Stick a bay leaf into each fig, place in a preserving jar, drizzle with port, and seal jar. Allow to stand for 6 hours at room temperature. Season goats' quark with sliced truffle, truffle oil, salt and white pepper. Lay out 4 sheets of filo pastry, brush with egg yoke, and lay remaining 4 sheets on top. Spread quark mixture in middle of 4 double sheets of pastry and roll up like a cone or cornet. Again brush with egg yoke, and bake in an oven preheated to 210 °C until golden. Serve at once on 4 plates, garnishing each pastry with a fig.

Serves 4

Ingredients
200 g fresh goats' quark
(curd cheese)
10 g white truffle
a few drops of white truffle oil
salt
8 sheets of ready-made filo
pastry
1 egg yoke for brushing
4 very ripe figs
4 bay leaves
2 tbsp port (red)

Ingredients
200 g coarse maize semolina
1 l water
20 g butter
salt
freshly grated nutmeg

plus
2 fresh robiola
(Italian curd cheese)
1 sprig of rosemary
30 ml best olive oil
coarse sea salt
cracked black pepper
40 g white truffle

Marinated robiola with polenta crust and white truffle

Add salt and butter to water and bring to the boil. Sprinkle in maize semolina and, stirring constantly, simmer for 1 $^1/_2$ hours – do not allow to catch on pan. Season polenta, and while still lukewarm pour over the fresh robiola. Leave to set, and then cut into slices 1 cm thick. Warm olive oil with a few rosemary spikes and drizzle over robiola slices. Sprinkle with coarse sea salt and freshly cracked black pepper. Finally, slice white truffle on top.

Serves 4

Castelmagno with truffle honey

Break up castelmagno into small pieces and drizzle with truffle honey. Sprinkle lightly toasted walnuts and white truffle over the cheese. A delicious cheese dish not to be missed at truffle time. Ill. p. 269.

Serves 4

Ingredients
250 g castelmagno or tuma cheese – about 60 g per person
80 g truffle honey (available in Piedmont at truffle time, or in various delicatessens)
10 g white truffle
30 g lightly toasted walnuts or pine kernels

Fonduta with white truffle

De-rind cheese and cut into 1-cm cubes. Macerate overnight in milk. Using a bain-marie, dissolve cheese cubes with butter and half the milk. Gradually stir in egg yokes until mixture thickens to a custard consistency. Season with grated nutmeg, and pour into soup bowls. Slice truffle over fonduta and serve.

A variation on this recipe is to lightly fry slices of white bread, rub them with a hint of garlic, put one bread slice in each soup bowl, lay a poached egg on it, and top with fonduta.

Serves 4–6

Ingredients
400 g fontina (Italian cheese from Aosta valley)
200 ml fresh milk
80 g knobs of butter
5 egg yokes
freshly grated nutmeg
60–80 g white truffle

... Ogni tanto alza
il (capo annusando
nell'aria: gli pare
che arrivi nell
buio una punta
di colore terroso,
tartufi ...

A truffle
is a truffle
is a truffle

"Homo mcdonaldis" probably knows this much about the truffle: it's a word with seven letters. The advanced eater even knows that there are two kinds – black and white.

But in fact there are many more. The generic Latin term "tuber" covers perhaps a dozen different truffles, of which only a few are of interest to the gourmet. Here is a brief overview of them.

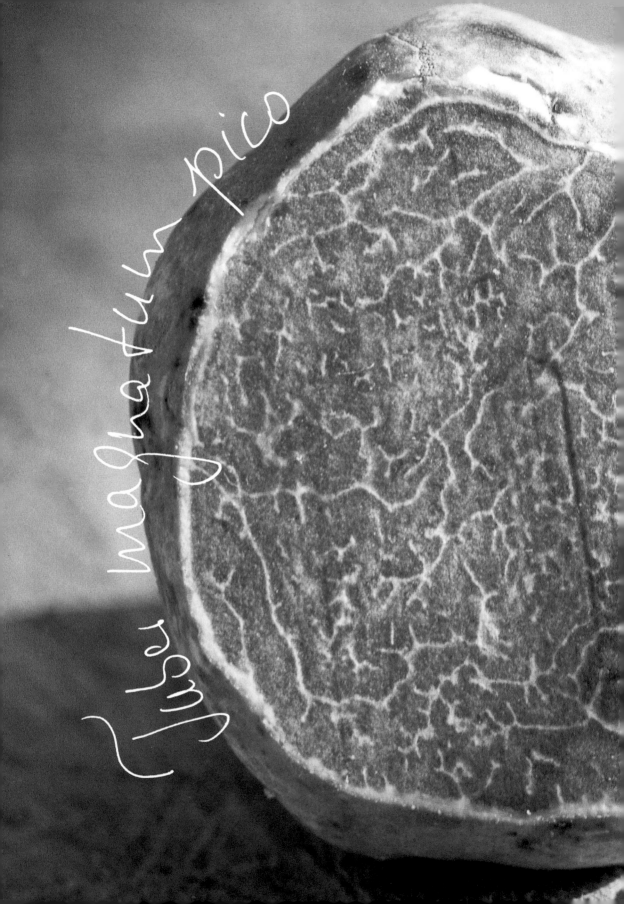

Tuba magnatum pico

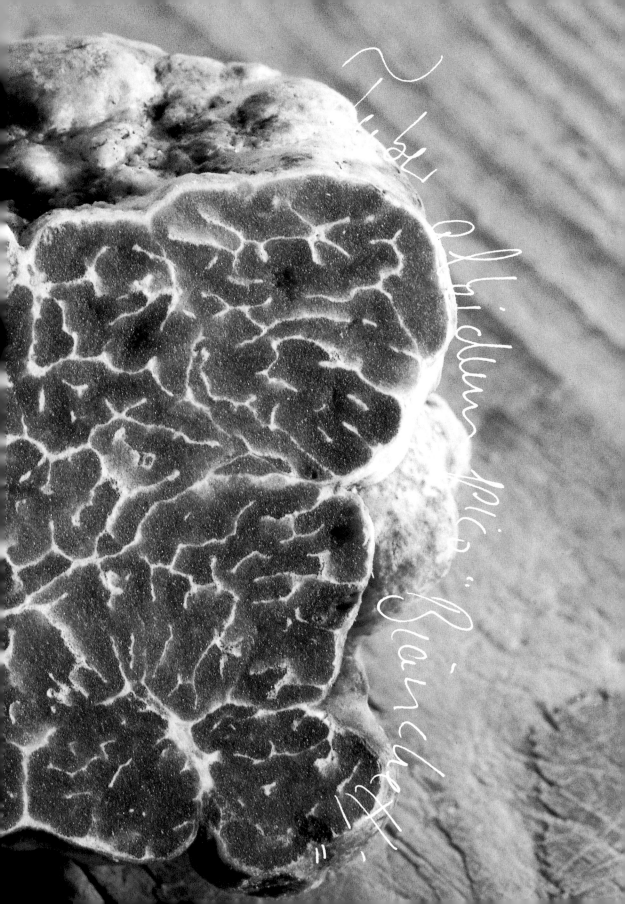

Tuber magnatum pico

The author is well-known as a francophile, and yet, faced with a choice, he would prefer a white truffle to a black one (even if it came from Périgord). Why? Well, of all truffles, tuber magnatum has the most alluring aroma and taste. Not everyone is of the same opinion. Thus in Piedmont, for example, it is forbidden to take magnatum into railway compartments on account of its powerful smell.

Magnatum reaches optimal maturity between late October and late December. On average, it weighs about 80g, but can reach as much as a kilo. It is brownish white and has a relatively smooth surface (peridium). The colour of the flesh varies depending on the host tree, but lies in the range nut to cream. All in all, this is the truffle variety in which the symbiotic partner is most strongly reflected. Thus the best specimens are harvested in the root system of oaks and lime trees. And unfortunately these stand only in Piedmont, with perhaps a few more in Lombardy, in the Veneto, Emilia Romagna and the Marches near Aqualagna. Annual production is currently a meagre 25 tons. Which makes it rare, and hence expensive – very very expensive. Tip: these truffles must be cut or sliced very thin, although if the slicer is set too fine, the truffle will smear and the taste will be lost. See ill. p. 272.

Tuber melanosporum vittadini

When ripe, it is deep black and varies in size between an egg and an apple. Its surface is covered with regular medium-sized warts, and once cut open reveals a black-violet flesh streaked with fine white veins. It reaches optimal ripeness between the end of November and March. If it has a reddish skin, it is not yet ripe and not worth the money.

Its aroma is strong and seductive. The "melanosporum" is commonly called the Périgord truffle, which is rather misleading, as this species is also found in even greater numbers in Spain as well as in Italy. Altogether about 75 tons of the black truffle are harvested. Those from France, and in particular from Périgord, command the highest prices. The principal production areas in Italy are Umbria (Spoleto, Norcia, L'Aquila) and the Marches (Aqualagna). A not inconsiderable part of this output goes towards satisfying the insatiable appetite of the French for the black truffle. See ill. p. 276.

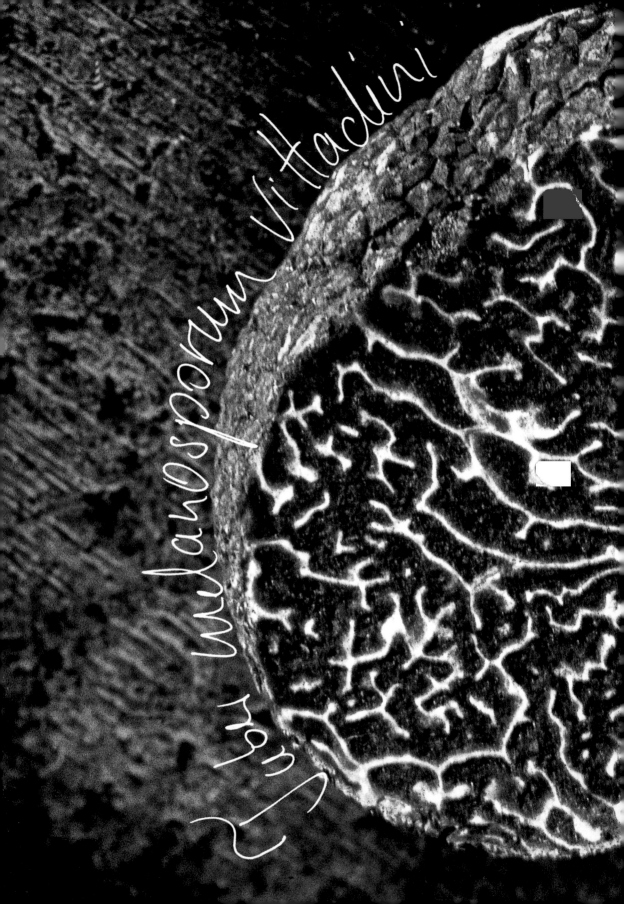

Tuber melanosporum vittadini

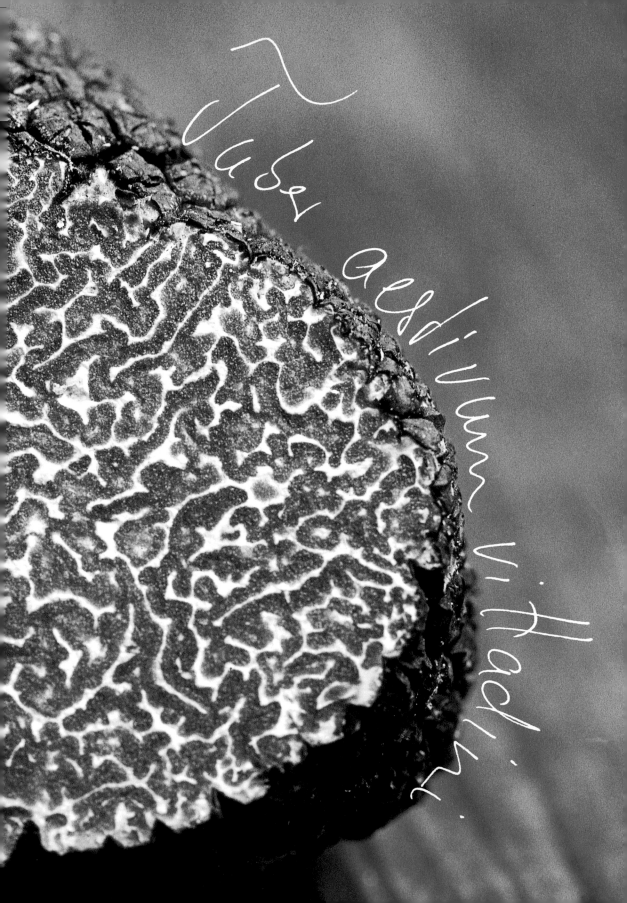

Tuba aestivum vittad.

The truffle – a matter of pride

A sniffy indifference characterizes most Italians and French when it comes to their respective neighbour's truffle regions. The Italians know only Périgord, and ignore the many other areas. The French mention the "magnatum", but then belittle it with observations such as "highly-prized by the Italians" or "very, very expensive", so that they do not have to get involved in a which-tastes-better competition.

Tuber aestivum vittadini

With a crop yield across Europe of 105 tons, this is the bulk deliverer among truffles. As its summery name implies, it is grubbed up out of the earth during the hot part of the year, revealing a black surface masking a yellowish beige interior. It is Europe's most widely distributed type of truffle, found mainly in Spain, France and Italy, but also in South Germany, especially around Baden. It is much cheaper, which, in view of its quality, seems justified (see ill. p. 277). Of significantly better quality is the

Tuber macrosporum vittadini

Its total production amounts to a princely 2 tons, making it virtually unobtainable commercially. It is reddish brown in appearance, almost smooth, small, and with a purple flesh. A genuine rarity, seen only in North Italy and even then only in private households. Not so valuable, but slightly more common is the

Tuber uncinatum

To what extent – if at all – it differs from the "aestivum" is a matter of dispute among experts. The Burgundians naturally insist that it is a distinct type of truffle and call it popularly "truffe de bourgogne". And this despite the fact that it cannot legally be called "truffle" at all. It can tolerate slightly colder conditions, which is why there have been attempts to cultivate it in Champagne and Lorraine. Delicious, but only when absolutely fresh. A truffle that excites more ambivalent feelings among truffle lovers is the

Tuber brumale vittadini

First, the good news. If you track down the real thing – not the "rufum" sub-type, which tastes horrible – the taste is not bad at all. Now for the bad news. Brumale is the spitting image of "melanosporum", and competes with it for living space. When truffle growers try to cultivate melanosporum, what they most fear is brumale. Thankfully it sometimes settles in as a "replacement tenant" at melanosporum's former host tree – rather like the morel, which is likewise found there as a successor. Finally, a few words about ...

Tuber albidum pico

Simply called "bianchetti" in Italy because of its white skin and small size. It grows from spring to early summer from Emilia Romagna down to roughly the latitude of Naples. It is considered the poor man's truffle, though the trade is making vigorous attempts to market it. However, with its pungent taste it is better used as a herb, even if dealers laud it more for its quality. See ill. p. 273.

Tuber rufum pico

Also called the red truffle, this lies heavy on the stomach. It is found throughout Italy, France and Spain, but is not traded. See ill. right.

Tuber excavatum vittadini

Owes its name to a hollow in its flesh, but is also known as the woody truffle. It tastes strongly of garlic and is hard to digest.

On balance, however, though you might sample the also-rans above for general edification or academic interest, the fact is – at the risk of sounding arrogant – that if you want to get on with eating truffles, go straight for magnatum and melanosporum.

Transportation and storage

Transportation and storage is a rather delicate matter. Truffles are up to 73% water and "lose their savour" i.e. shrink by about 5% of bodyweight per day – a reason to slow down the loss by any means possible:

You wrap the truffle in kitchen paper, close it in an air-tight jar, and put it in the fridge. The paper should be changed at least once a day, so that the truffle stays dry and does not go mouldy or bad.

An old but effective strategy is to dip the truffle in wax. In this way neither moisture nor aroma can escape. A method used in the 16th century to bring the white delicacies intact from Italy to the French court. Both white and black truffles can be kept from three days to a week. But they taste best completely fresh.

...A quest'ora ciascuno dovrebbe fermasi
per la strada e guardare come tutto maturi.
C'è persino una brezza, che non smuove
le nubi, ma che basta dirigere il fumo
azzurino senza romperlo: è un nuovo sapore
che passa. E il tabacco va intinto di grappa.
E così che le donne non saranno le sole
a godere il mattino.

Bibliography:

Colette
Prisons et paradis (pp. 3, 156, 233)
© Librairie Arthème Fayard, Paris, 1986

Cesare Pavese
La Luna e I Falio (p. 116)
© Giulio Einaudi Editori, Milan, 1950

Cesare Pavese
Racconti (pp. 94, 268)
© Giulio Einaudi Editori, Milan, 1961

Cesare Pavese
Poesie (p. 284)
© Giulio Einaudi Editori, Milan, 1961

Translation of the texts by
Gabriele-Sidonie Colette and Cesare Pavese

Page 3:   Between the moment when the casserole, cauldron, or saucepan is placed on the flame, and that other moment of the anxious pleasure and voluptuous hope when, at table, you lift the lid on a steaming dish, everything is sorcery, mystery and transmutation.

Page 42:   And they returned home tired and dirty, but laden with partridges, hares and game.

Page 94:   ...just knowing certain tings can make you happy...

Page 116: I imagined seeing the women grating, kneading the dough, preparing the feast, stoking the fire; and my tongue could almost taste their fare...

Page 156: Where I come from, during a good meal, you don't get 'thirsty' but 'hungry for drink'...

Page 233: Of all black princesses, this is the most capricious, the most revered. It costs it weight in gold.

Page 268: Now and then he raises his head and sniffs the air: there in the darkness, he seems to catch the scent of freshly dug earth, of freshly uncovered truffles.

Page 284: At this hour everyone should stop on his way and look at nature growing round about.
There is a breeze too, which leaves the clouds unruffled, but gently prods the bluish haze
formed by a fresh scent passing by, without dispersing it.
It is the smell of tobacco replete with Grappa.
Which makes the morning a time
not just for the enjoyment of the womenfollk.

Illustrations:

Acknowledgements

We would like to thank Mariuccia and Piercarlo
Ferrero of the San Marco restaurant in Canelli
for their generous friendship, patience and
advice. Thanks also to Carlo Marmo, not just an
indefatigable companion, but since those days a
friend for life.
We are much indebted to Tine and Hannes, who
so naturally put at our disposal their kitchen,
home and garden in Périgord.
Sincere thanks are also due to the following for
their help, cooperation and hospitality: Carlo
Prazzi, Roberto Scarsi, Ferdinando Marino,
Giovanni and Gian Paolo-die Trifülau, Domenico,
Piero Balestrino, the Cooperativa in Cossano
Belbo, the Gruppo Urbani Tartufi in San Anatolia
di Narco, Claude Lalot in Sainte Alvère, and
Robert Pouliquen in Bergerac.
Lastly we wish to express our thanks to all those
who directly or indirectly have helped with the
realization of this book.